1998

JOHN DEWEY

SUNY Series, The Philosophy of Education

Philip L. Smith, Editor

JOHN DEWEY

RETHINKING OUR TIME

☙❦❧

Raymond D. Boisvert

State University of New York Press

Cover photograph: John Dewey's Ninetieth Birthday Celebration, New York Waldorf Astoria Hotel, 1949. Courtesy of John Dewey Papers, Special Collections/Morris Library, Southern Illinois University at Carbondale.

Cover production: Christine Muran

Published by
State University of New York Press, Albany

For information, address State University of New York Press, State University Plaza, Albany, N.Y. 12246

Production by M. R. Mulholland
Marketing by Fran Keneston

Library of Congress Cataloging-in-Publication Data

Boisvert, Raymond D.
    John Dewey : rethinking our time / Raymond D. Boisvert.
        p.   cm. — (SUNY series, the philosophy of education)
    Includes bibliographical references and index.
    ISBN 0-7914-3529-6 (hard : alk. paper). — ISBN 0-7914-3530-X (pbk. : alk. paper)
    1. Dewey, John, 1854–1952. I. Title. II. Series: SUNY series in philosophy of education.
    B945.D4B65 1997
    191—dc 21   96-52291
                                                                       CIP

10   9   8   7   6   5   4   3   2   1

For Jayne

Que tout ce qu'on entend, l'on voit ou l'on respire,
Tout dise: "Ils ont aimés!"
                                    Lamartine, Le Lac

Contents

Illustrations

Acknowledgments

Everyone who works on John Dewey's philosophy owes a great debt of gratitude to Jo Ann Boydston for her editorial efforts in bringing out the thirty-seven volumes of Dewey's collected works. This marvelous collection, together with the index, is not only an indispensable tool for the scholar, but is also helping make Dewey's thought central to American culture once again.

Several of the chapters in this book were initially prepared and presented during a year spent in France as a Fulbright scholar. I am grateful to my hosts at the University of Lyon II for the opportunity to teach American Studies in their institution. The philosophy department at the neighboring University of Lyon III was kind enough to extend me an invitation to lecture there. The ideas for the introduction to the present book were first formulated in that lecture.

The most stimulating part of my year in France was spent at the University of Perpignan's *Institut de Recherche en Sciences de la Communication et de l'Éducation* founded by the great Dewey and Peirce scholar Gérard Deledalle. For inspiration, intellectual stimulation, and warm hospitality, I am grateful to him and to his colleagues, especially Joelle Rethoré, Tony Jappy, Michel Balat, Jean-Pierre Kaminker, and Werner Burzlaff.

Chapter 5 has already appeared, in a slightly different form, in *Studies in Philosophy and Education* 13 (1994–95): 325–41. It is reprinted with the permission of Kluwer Academic Publishers. The photos of John Dewey appear with the permission of the John Dewey Papers, Special Collections/Morris Library, Southern Illinois University at Carbondale.

For tracking down references and helping me access difficult to find material, I am grateful to Sean Maloney and John Vallely of the Siena College library. I am also indebted to Sue Kuebler for secretarial help, and to Ellen Johnson for meticulous care in preparing the final draft.

Siena College provided me with two summer research stipends for work related to this book. I wish to express my gratitude to two deans who were constantly encouraging and supportive of my research, Tom Bulger and Lois Daly. My thanks also to Dr. Douglas Astolfi, former Vice-President for Academic Affairs at Siena College, through whose initiative new programs in support of faculty research and writing have been implemented.

Raymond D. Boisvert

Loudonville, New York
Five Islands, Maine

Introduction

The "Naissance" and "Renaissance"
of American Philosophy

A visitor to the United States in the 1830s may well have considered it to be an intellectual wasteland. One of America's leading lights, Ralph Waldo Emerson, seemed to admit as much when he asked, in an 1836 journal entry, why "there is no genius in the Arts in this country" (Allen, 285). After spending parts of 1831 and 1832 in the United States, a now famous visitor was led to comment on the country's almost total lack of philosophical curiosity. "I think," wrote Tocqueville, "that in no country in the civilized world is less attention paid to philosophy than in the United States" (De Tocqueville, 143).

Within a generation, the literary output of the new nation would respond to Emerson's question by revealing some genius in the literary arts. Emerson's own essay *Nature* came out in 1836, and Poe's *Tales of the Grotesque and Arabesque* in 1840. The decade of the '50s opened with Hawthorne's *The Scarlet Letter*, followed quickly (1851) by Melville's *Moby-Dick*, Thoreau's *Walden* (1854), and Whitman's *Leaves of Grass* (1855).

It took a little longer for the philosophical muse to be heard. Religious and political questions had occasioned quasi-philosophical reflection and writing since before the Declaration of Independence. But the emergence of individuals for whom the whole panoply of philosophical questions could be worn with ease did not come until the generation which followed that of Emerson and Hawthorne. The births of these thinkers coincided with the literary renaissance of the mid-nineteenth century: Charles Sanders Peirce (1839), William James (1842), Josiah Royce (1855), John Dewey (1859), and George Herbert Mead (1862). Their writings began to appear in the last third of the 1800s. Worldwide recognition came with the opening of the new century.

As if to signal the rising prominence of American philosophy in the 1900s, the new century's opening was marked by the invitation of an American to a prestigious European lectureship. Josiah Royce's *The World and the Individual* was first delivered as the Gifford lectures at the University of Aberdeen in 1899–1900. He was followed by William James, whose international fame was greater even than that of Royce.

These two invitations marked an important turning point in American philosophy. Until then the United States had continued to be, intellectually at least, a colony. The springs of generative ideas were located in Europe. Eventually, the ideas made their way across the Atlantic where they were eagerly awaited. James admitted as much when he addressed his Scottish audience in 1901: "To us Americans, the experience of receiving instruction from the living voice, as well as from the books, of European scholars, is very familiar. . . . It seems the natural thing for us to listen whilst the Europeans talk."

The invitation to deliver the lectures had made of him a pioneer, an aspect of the situation he found daunting. "The contrary habit, of talking whilst Europeans listen, we have not yet acquired; and in him who first makes the adventure it begets a certain sense of apology being due for so presumptuous an act." Nonetheless, James was clearly pleased, and expressed his aspiration that the flow of ideas would now move both ways across the Atlantic. "Let me say only this, that now that the current, here and at Aberdeen, has begun to run from west to east, I hope it may continue to do so" (James, 1985, 11–12).

James's writings and those of his younger colleague, John Dewey, helped to insure that the flow of ideas would move not only in two directions across the Atlantic, but across the Pacific as well. Twenty-eight years after James's Gifford lectures, it was Dewey's turn to take the podium at the University of Edinburgh to deliver a series of talks which would become *The Quest for Certainty*. By this time, his fame had eclipsed even that of James. Dewey had already been invited to the Imperial University at Tokyo in 1919. He spent the academic years 1919–20 and 1920–21 in China, having been the "first major western scholar to visit at the invitation of the Chinese" (Rockefeller, 358). His hosts even conferred an honorary degree on Dewey, referring to him as the "second Confucius" (Dykhuizen, 197).

Had De Tocqueville been able to return 100 years later, he would have been astounded by the altered intellectual climate. In 1930, almost exactly a century after his trip, the most prominent university in De Tocqueville's home country recognized this changed climate by conferring an honorary degree on John Dewey. On November 6, the day before he received the Sorbonne degree, Dewey read a paper, "Three Independent Factors in Morals," to a select group of Parisian philosophers. When Leon Robin, Marcel Mauss, Jean Wahl, and Xavier Leon praised the American philosopher and acknowledged his influence, ("your philosophy has claimed the attention of thinkers in France for quite a long time") (LW 5:497) the 1830s evaluation of America's intellectual poverty could be finally laid to rest.[1]

By the end of the next year, 1931, death had taken all of the seminal American philosophers but one, John Dewey. On the international stage, the world would soon be involved in another war. The Second World War is important for philosophy in the United States because of an ironic inversion. America emerged from the war as the preeminent economic and military world power. For philosophy, however, the postwar period was one of recolonization. The classical American philosophers were quickly marginalized as universities sought to embrace the latest European ideas.

Positivism and existentialism were imported from the continent, and language analysis from the British Isles. By the time Dewey died in 1952, America was well on its way to forgetting its indigenous thinkers born in the 1800s.[2] Philosophy in America would continue to thrive, but in directions that were hostile to the very conceptions of philosophy that motivated people like Royce, James, and Dewey. Names like Rudolf Carnap, Moritz Schlick, Jean-Paul Sartre, Bertrand Russell, G. E. Moore, Martin Heidegger, and J. L. Austin began to fill academic syllabi. Their appearance could have been a welcome stimulus in its interaction with the native philosophy. Unfortunately, the academics who embraced them too often took on the role of imperialists seeking a thorough recolonization of the American territory.

During the 1970s the situation began once again to change. In 1969, under the editorship of Jo Ann Boydston, Southern Illinois University Press brought out the first of a projected thirty-seven volumes of Dewey's works. Now completed, the collection has been praised as one of "the finest editions of the collected works of an American author" (Westbrook, 555). Its publication, making Dewey's writings easily available, was both a boon to researchers and a catalyst for renewed interest in his thought.

Soon after the inauguration of the Dewey edition, a small group of scholars founded, in 1973, the Society for the

Advancement of American Philosophy, dedicated to the preservation and resurrection of classical American thought. Their
work was given a great boost by someone whose interests in
classical American thinkers was beginning to burgeon at the
same time. Richard Rorty's impact was all the more significant
since he had been a recognized member of the philosophical
establishment which disdained classical American thinkers. His
presidential address to the Eastern Division of the American
Philosophical Association in 1979, together with his *Philosophy
and the Mirror of Nature* (1979) and *Consequences of Pragmatism*
(1982), helped bring classical American philosophy in general,
and the thought of John Dewey in particular, to the forefront of
discussion.

The presidential address, referring to James and Dewey,
had claimed that "at present, however, these two writers are
neglected" (Rorty, 1982, 160). Thanks to Rorty, to the Dewey
edition, and to the Society for the Advancement of American
Philosophy, that is no longer the case. On Dewey alone, there has
been prodigious publication in the '80s and '90s.[3]

The present book seeks to play a special role in this revival.
Reviving a now little-used term, I would describe the text as a
"primer." Its aim is to serve as a brief and generally accessible
introduction to Dewey's philosophy. The topics chosen for elaboration have been selected as central to an inclusive overview of
his positions. The presentation, it is hoped, will be lucid without
distorting the complexity of Deweyan formulations. Because of its
aim and its limited length, the text is expository rather than critical. It attempts to articulate a sympathetic interpretation of
Dewey's thought.[4] If contemporary readers are drawn to the
Deweyan corpus, and, through it, stimulated, not to mere repetition, but to novel articulations, then the aim of this little book
will have been met.

Dewey's Reconstruction of the Tradition

Dewey sought above all else to be a productive, constructive
philosopher. He tried to do justice to a comprehensive grasp of
experience that stressed the continuity between nature and culture. He did as much as anyone in the twentieth century to re-
vitalize democratic aspirations and provide them with philosophical ballast. Unlike philosophers who think of themselves as
the atemporal voice of Being itself, Dewey unapologetically wrote

from his own time and for it.⁵ The sources of inspiration on which he drew were wide-ranging. They were not only contemporary and Modern. They were pre-Modern as well. (The term "modern" is ambiguous. In ordinary parlance it is roughly synonymous with the contemporary period. Within the context of intellectual history, however, it indicates a particular period now thought to have come to a close (1600–1900). This latter is the sense in which I will be using the term. To indicate this, I am spelling it with an uppercase "M.") In order best to speak to his own time, he was irenic in welcoming varied sources of inspiration. This is why, as I explain in the conclusion, the best label for Dewey can be neither "Modern" nor "postmodern." He was rather, in the term introduced by Bruno Latour, "polytemporal" in attitude.

Naturally, as a creative thinker, he did not draw uncritically from these sources. What he did, to his credit, was to sort out overstatements, one-sided emphases, erroneous biases, and archaic formulations, from the living contributions made by philosophers in the tradition. Very rarely, Kant may be an exception, did Dewey pronounce blanket condemnations. He wished resolutely to speak to the present. Doing so in a constructive, productive fashion necessitated drawing on what was best from the past.

His incorporation of philosophy's history, was not, however, haphazard. He spoke explicitly of the need for "Reconstruction in Philosophy," the title he gave to one of his most popular books. This reconstruction was to be undertaken from a particular perspective. While some strands from the tradition were to be woven into the new fabric, others were to be left out. Perhaps an appropriate way to begin, then, is by providing a brief outline of the strands from which Dewey disassociated himself. I identify three of these which will reappear in various guises throughout my analysis: the Plotinian Temptation, the Galilean Purification, and the Asomatic Attitude.

The Plotinian Temptation

The philosophy of the Greeks, it could be argued, was initially passed on to the West via the distorting lenses of St. Augustine (354–430), lenses ground and shaped by a thinker whose influence on him had been decisive, Plotinus (205–270).Whereas Plato in the *Timaeus* had posited three ultimate principles to explain existence, the Demiurge, the Forms, and Matter, Plotinus explained all of existence as an emanation from the "One," his highest principle. Whereas for Plato the idea of "Good" had been a central motivating concern, penetrating everywhere like sunlight, for Plotinus the ideal of life was an escape from the multiple and material world of the here and now. The new aim was that of effecting a return to the One which was the source of all.

The ideal of a unity as both underlying the complexity of existence and serving as the ultimate end of life has had a controlling influence in much of Western thought. One plot, replayed in diverse ways, has been that of overcoming multiplicity in order to arrive at the underlying reality. From the Cartesian cogitations seeking a single, irrecusable idea, to the simple sense data of Locke, the atoms of Dalton, the linguistic search for an *Ursprache*, through the twentieth-century writings praising the unity exemplified in the *fasces*, the Roman symbol adapted by Mussolini to symbolize the unity of the nation, philosophers have been attracted by oneness, if not as an absolute ideal, then certainly as a regulative one.

The Plotinian Temptation to assert unity as both ground and goal is not one to which Dewey succumbs. In the speech delivered to Parisian philosophers, he asserted, characteristically, that morality cannot be reduced to any of the single guiding principles selected as ultimate by moral philosophers: the culmination of natural desires, the demands of duty, or the dialectic of sympathy and antipathy. There are, as Dewey put it, "three independent factors in morals" not three competitors for the one ultimate principle.

Recently, this Deweyan "cluster" approach has been revived by a philosopher who seems wholly outside the influence of classical American philosophy. Martha Nussbaum's sensitive reading of Greek tragedy leads her to side with the tragedians when they recognize how an irreducible plurality of commitments is an ineluctable component of human life. Philosophers, by contrast, have often attempted to deny the ineluctability of this condition by claiming that "really" only a single aim or end is *the* correct one. "At most one can be true: the other can and should be discarded as false, therefore no longer relevant" (Nussbaum, 30). Dewey, it seems to me, would also side with the tragedians in accepting a central element of Greek theology: "the idea that the gods impose upon mortals divergent and even conflicting requirements" (Nussbaum, 30).[6]

At the basis of Deweyan philosophy is always an analogous set of clusters whose components we must struggle to hold together in a homeostatic balance. Those who succumb to the Plotinian Temptation reject the ultimacy of the cluster, and seek a deeper *unity*. Dewey, admitting the irreducible nature of multiplicity, seeks *harmony*. He is the anti-Plotinus. For him pluralism goes all the way down.

The Galilean Purification

Post-medieval philosophy, "Modern" philosophy, developed in conjunction with great advances in science. So powerful was the influence of science, that Ortega y Gasset has claimed that Modern philosophy was "cross-eyed," keeping one eye on experience, the other on the discoveries of the sciences (Ortega y Gasset, 34). Dewey never wavered in his support of the sciences and in his rejection of any philosophic view that denigrated their accomplishments. Nonetheless, he did turn away from a methodological procedure made prominent by Galileo and taken over by various philosophers.

The genius of Galileo, allowing him to move beyond Aristotelian science, lay in his willingness to substitute an idealized situation for the clumsy, muddled context provided by ordinary experience. The Galilean advance depended on a profound imaginative leap, considering the acceleration of moving objects when ideal conditions were substituted for ordinary ones.

As Alexandre Koyré put it, Galileo's success was based on his ability to explain "that which *exists* by reference to that which *does not exist*, which never exists, by reference even to that which *never could exist*" (Koyré, 155). Salviati, the character representing Galileo in his *Dialogue Concerning the Two Chief World Systems*, tries to explain this procedure to the more simple-minded Simplicio, who represents common sense: "Now how long would the ball continue to roll, and how fast? Remember that I said a perfectly round ball and a highly polished surface, in order to remove all external and accidental impediments. Similarly I want you to take away any impediment of the air caused by its resistance to separation, and all other accidental obstacles, if there are any" (Koyre, 167).

Without such a bold shift in approach to the questions of science, we might never have come to the realization that, with respect to gravitation, the fall of a feather is the same as that of a cannon ball. The Galilean Purification, removing ourselves from ordinary experience and substituting an alternative context, was indispensable to progress in science. But, despite their indeterminate commingling in Greek thought, philosophy and science have been, since the Renaissance, quite different, even if related, studies. Philosophy is inextricably involved with the search for the good life. As such, it must welcome and learn from the discoveries made by scientists. This does not mean, however, that philosophy and science coalesce into an indistinguishable activity.

Science concentrates on describing the elemental structures of things for purposes of prediction and control. The Galilean Purification was a *sine qua non* for scientific advance. It is, however, uncongenial to philosophy which begins and ends in ordinary lived experience. In spite of this, many Modern philosophers simply took for granted the need for a Galilean Purification in their own field as well. Unhappy with the complex messiness of ordinary experience, they sought to ground philosophy in a purer starting point.

Rene Descartes (1596–1650) undertook a version of the Galilean Purification. He refused to philosophize until he had suspended:

1.   the evidence of his senses,
2.   the intellectual tradition in which he had been schooled, and
3.   the direct experience of his travels.

Only after these purifications could he arrive at his apodictic first principle "I think therefore I am." Descartes's *Discourse* and his *Meditations* refuse the immediate present as the appropriate starting point for reflection. They begin with a rigorous, self-conscious purification, the projection of an ideal situation within which philosophizing can begin.

Francis Bacon's (1561–1626) purifying move is revealed in his longing for a world free of our natural and cultural inheritances, the so-called four "idols." Only in such an idealized world could we directly confront the real. But in so doing we transform ourselves into something which we are not, and which we can probably never be: individuals whose language has no limitations, who can step outside of their unique perspectives, who do not depend on inherited systems of thought, and who have no prejudices. Locke and Rousseau extended the Galilean strategy into the seventeenth and eighteenth centuries when they projected humans into an imaginary, original state of nature. More recently John Rawls's invention of an "original situation" reveals the lingering influence of the Galilean Purification.

Dewey, although a descendant of the Puritans, does not continue this Modern fetish with purity. Philosophical analysis always begins *in medias res*. The here and now is not something to be overcome. It is rather that which sets the issues and problems that have to be considered, as well as the actual conditions within which alternatives can be projected. The context of ordinary experience is also the locus to which we must return if philosophy is going to have any impact in helping bring about a good life.

The stand taken here by Dewey is analogous to that taken in Anglo-American philosophy by those who rejected the siren song of ideal languages. Such languages, cleansed of muddled phrasings, ambiguities, and vagueness, were the linguistic manifestation of Galileo's drive to purify. In this respect, Dewey's naturalism has more in common with the Wittgenstein of the *Investigations* than with the author of the *Tractatus*.[7]

To follow Dewey we need not disdain everyday existence. Philosophy is at home in the concrete, complex, indeed messy, condition of human life. If it is to be successful, philosophical reflection must remain alert to this condition. No attempt is to be made to begin reflection from an artificial, unreal, make-believe starting point. Philosophy need not be cross-eyed. It needs to welcome, encourage, and defend science. At the same time, it needs to embrace its own point of departure, not attempt to appropriate one which, while successful in physics, is inimical to philosophy's own aims.

The Asomatic Attitude

Plotinus, we are told, held such disdain for the body that he refused to have his picture painted. Descartes, some 1,400 years later, codified the separation of mind from body as a cornerstone of Modern thought. Philosophy was to be "rational" and rationality was defined in terms of a mind opposed to the body. Such ordinary dimensions of human life as the emotions had to be suppressed because they were deemed a one-dimensional clouding of clear thought. The disembodied ideal reached a crescendo of sorts in the thought of Immanuel Kant (1724–1804), who articulated a *Critique of Pure Reason*. The purity of reason became a controlling ideal for philosophers. Humans were defined as "thinking things" (Descartes) or as "rational essences" (Kant). The body, when considered at all, was interpreted as a clumsy, inconvenient, and troublesome appendage. This had not always been the preeminent position in philosophy. The Greek tradition, for example, included some outright dualists like Pythagoras, but others, like Aristotle and the tragedians, tended to emphasize ways in which the mental and the somatic were inextricably linked.[8]

Dewey will have none of the Modern bicompartmentalization of human beings. His great enemy was dualism. He rooted it out in all of its forms. Education, for example, was not for him a mere matter of getting information to the mind. Children could not learn optimally unless they were active, using their hands and engaging in varied sorts of experimentations. Teachers could not teach effectively if they thought of themselves as information machines passing on data from one mind to the next. They too had to be physically active, moving around to stimulate the students as human beings, not just as disembodied minds.

Knowledge does not derive from some asomatic "reason" but from embodied "intelligence." The good life is not that of withdrawal, escape from the body in order to achieve inner purification. Here again the analyses of Nussbaum resonate with Deweyan themes. An Aristotelian, she asserts (and, as this book will show, Dewey was in many ways Aristotelian in outlook), will not cut off the passions in favor of an "acute scientific intelligence." To do so would be to "miss a lot that is relevant for practice and be inhumanly cut off from much of the value of our lives" (Nussbaum, 310). Dewey would agree wholeheartedly. Human, embodied experiencing is not a matter of receiving data into a mental computer. It involves a fully human response to the environment within which we are enmeshed.

Dewey's writings challenge us to reconstruct philosophy apart from the Plotinian Temptation, the Galilean Purification, and the Asomatic Attitude. The Plotinian Temptation urges us to reject pluralism as illusory and seek unity as our highest goal. Dewey admits the irreducibility of pluralism and sets harmony, not unity, as the appropriate human ideal. The Galilean Purification suggests an artificial stance as the appropriate starting point. For Dewey, philosophical reflection must grow out of the muddled, ambiguous, lived present. The Asomatic Attitude isolates mind from body. Deweyan philosophy is a philosophy for humans, embodied individuals endowed with intelligence.

Only by recognizing these fundamental differences with the tradition can we begin to appreciate Dewey's reconstruction in philosophy. That reconstruction touched on all areas of philosophical importance: human experience, knowledge, social/moral issues, education, art, politics, and religion. The chapters which follow seek to explore Dewey's formulations in these areas.

In that exploration, I have tried to stress the meaning and purpose of Dewey's thought. This meaning has been mired in controversies as a result of several unfortunate terminological appropriations by Dewey. Recognizing this, Dewey himself, late in his career, tended to avoid these terms. In the preface to *Logic: The Theory of Inquiry*, for example, he explained why the most famous of them, "pragmatism," was missing from his text.

> The word "Pragmatism" does not, I think, occur in the text. Perhaps the word lends itself to misconception. At all events, so much misunderstanding and relatively futile controversy have gathered about the word that it seemed advisable to avoid its use (LW 12:4).

The substance of his position was not affected. It was in order to present that substance more effectively that Dewey refrained from using the very word by which his philosophical position was popularly identified.

Following Dewey's example, I have made scarce use of terminological lightning rods like "pragmatism," "instrumentalism," "scientific method," and "problematic situation." Such terms and expressions tend to be immediately incorporated into semantic landscapes that are alien to Dewey's endeavor. They thus obfuscate rather than clarify his positions. My attempt has been to bring out the substance and sense of Dewey's philosophy in a language less susceptible to misconstrual.

Freed of "futile" controversies engendered by overused labels, my hope is that Dewey will be reread for the single most important reason for which any philosopher is read: because he sheds light on the issues that dominate our own time. We, like Dewey, find ourselves moving into a new century. Like him, we wonder how to realize democratic aspirations in a large, technologically advanced, multi-ethnic society. We worry about the inadequacy of our schools, and seek for ways to resolve the tensions between big business, big government, and the public interest. The problems of incorporating the discoveries of the sciences with the everyday search for the good life, of overcoming the disjunction between art and ordinary life, and of sorting out the opposition between an overly rationalized secularism and a closed-minded religiosity, are as real today as they were in Dewey's time.[9]

The present revival of interest in Dewey results in great part because his concerns are also our concerns. Few philosophers have spoken to their times in as comprehensive a way as has Dewey. If the present book provides a flavor of that comprehensiveness and a taste for the original texts, it will have accomplished its purpose.

1

The Life-World

Lived Experience

A contemporary of Dewey's, the prominent British philosopher Bertrand Russell (1872–1970), began one of his most popular books by distinguishing "sense data" (that which is grasped by the senses), from "sensation," the awareness that we are experiencing sense data (Russell, 12). Philosophy originates, for Russell, with the careful description of basic experiences, such as that of a table. "To the eye it is oblong, brown and shiny, to the touch it is smooth and cool and hard; when I tap it, it gives out a wooden sound" (Russell, 9). Such a procedure, starting with sense data, had become standard practice in the tradition of British Empiricism. Philosophers were expected to begin by identifying the elemental building blocks of experience. Their next task was to explain the emergence of ideas from these foundational units. Finally, they had to explain how ideas, thus engendered, were related to the external world.

A literary figure born one year before Russell, writing a new sort of novel, offered a different perspective on the nature of experience. When Marcel Proust (1871–1922) recalled the *petite madeleine* soaked in a spoonful of tea, his description had nothing of the cold enumeration of sense impressions that marked Russell's reaction to the table. Proust first described the context that prepared his experience: a cold day, surly mood, boredom, his mother's surprising offer of tea which he rarely drank.

> And soon, mechanically, weary after a dull day with the prospect of a depressing morrow, I raised to my lips a spoonful of the tea in which I had soaked a morsel of the cake. No sooner had the warm liquid, and the crumbs with it, touched my palate than a shudder ran through my whole body, and I stopped, intent upon the extraordinary changes that were taking place. (Proust, 54–55)

Eventually, Proust comes to realize that the experience of the tea-soaked madeleine awakened memories of his Aunt Léonie, who used to give him a just such a morsel after Sunday mass. In turn, this set off a train of memories that is one of the literary masterpieces of the twentieth century.

Understanding the nature of experience is no small matter when trying to grasp a philosophical position. John Smith has correctly pointed out that "the reconstruction of experience by the Pragmatists" is "their most important contribution" (Smith, 1992, 17). The contrast between experience as sense data in Russell, and experience as historically and contextually conditioned in Proust, will help us to understand the point of departure for Dewey. "Experience," in Dewey's writings is meant to articulate the inclusive, multi-faceted, that is to say fully human, modes of prehending, reacting to, and interacting with our surroundings. Because, for him, "experience" identifies the mode of human being-in-the-world, Dewey's understanding of it is actually closer to that of the novelist Proust than to that of his fellow philosopher Russell.

Dewey cannot, however, follow Proust, who, after a rich elaboration of his "experience," retreats to his inner self. "I put down my cup and examine my own mind" (Proust, 55). Both Russell and Proust, although initially tethered to their surroundings, soon lose sight of these. The first transforms the life-world into a series of "objective" data that have little to do with the everyday use and enjoyment we make of that world. The second distances himself from immersion in the here and now. His escape is into a "subjective" re-creation of the past.

Deweyan "empirical naturalism" (LW 1:4) combines the multifaceted sensitivity of a Proust with the concern for the here and now of a Russell. Philosophers are, after all, ordinary human beings. They are neither cold, objective accumulators of data, nor detached, subjective revelers in the past. Traditional empiricism, stressing the importance of experience, had taken philosophy in a positive direction. However, representatives of the tradition, like Russell, do not actually begin with ordinary human experience. What they present as fundamental "givens" are really results of a prior Galilean Purification. Such results might best be described, not as "givens" but as "takens." Empiricists, we might say, were not sufficiently empirical.

Ordinary human experience, marked as it is by a qualitative dimension, by affect and memory, by definite interests, is distorted in the reductive empiricism espoused by Russell. The reduction strips away the multiple dimensions of fully human experiencing. What remains are the senses as free-floating receptors working in isolation. The percepta apprehended by these senses are then misleadingly read back into the original context as raw, initial data.

Such a procedure is akin to a linguist claiming that first there were individual letters, then words, then grammar, and finally language. The actual empirical primacy of a living language is dismissed in favor of what has emerged from second-order activities of analysis and abstraction. Analysis and abstraction can isolate and construe elemental units within a language. These *results* should not, however, be read back into the situation as original existential data.

In his introductory chapter to *Experience and Nature* Dewey cites an unnamed philosopher's description of a chair, one analogous to Russell's description of the table. Such a description is revealed to be a model of misconstruing ordinary experience. It embodies two major defects:

1. Experience "is reduced to the traits connected with the *act of experiencing*, in this case the act of seeing."
2. "The other point is that, even in such a brief statement as that just quoted, there is compelled recognition of an *object* of experience which is infinitely other and more than what is asserted to be alone experienced." (LW 1:25)

Proust's experience of the madeleine provides some sense of what is the "infinitely other and more" referred to by Dewey in his criticism of the traditional empiricist construction of experience. The proper starting point for philosophy should be full, concrete human experiencing. There is no need for a Galilean reduction. Human experience, as in Proust, is saturated with memory and affect. The tea-soaked madeleine is a nexus of meaning far surpassing, "infinitely other" as Dewey puts it, the description in terms of sense data.

All of this is important because it helps identify an absolutely crucial difference between Deweyan philosophizing and that of alternative traditions. Philosophies which seize upon different points of departure will be dramatically divergent in their fully worked-out forms. Rather than construe an artificially purified situation, Dewey simply accepts that, although philosophy grows beyond ordinary, lived experience, that is where it must begin.

The first edition of *Experience and Nature* had used strong language to indicate the self-defeating nature of following the Galilean Purification. Philosophers who would substitute products of subsequent abstractive refinement for the "obvious and immediate facts of gross experience," are "unmindful that thereby philosophy itself commits suicide" (LW 1:366–67). History teaches us that philosophers are tempted to "substitute ratiocination and its conclusions for things that are done, suffered and imagined." They "are wont to start with highly simplified premises." This moment, what I have called the Galilean Purification, is undertaken quite consciously. Philosophers have set as their goals "absolute certainty in knowledge of things and absolute security in the ordering of life." Having such goals in mind, they chose initial data and principles "sufficiently simple to yield what is sought" (LW 1:373). This procedure may be self-reinforcing, but it is neither empirical nor fruitful in dealing with actual lived experience.

Unlike the philosophers he criticizes, Dewey does not begin with a prior commitment to achieving absolute certainty. Human knowing is provisional, incomplete, and probabilistic. We rarely act with the absolute security that our choices are *the* absolutely appropriate ones. This is neither cause for despair nor for seeking out artificial forms of security. The human condition, in its fullness, must be taken into account by the philosopher. Experience is what can open the fullness of that condition to us.

Accepting neither the Galilean Purification nor the Asomatic Attitude, Deweyan philosophizing, like that of Charles S. Peirce before him,[1] begins where humans actually find themselves, in the here and now of lived experience. Genuine empirical method in philosophy, Dewey claims, "cautions us that we must begin with things in their complex entanglements rather than with simplifications made for the purpose of effective judgment and action" (LW 1:387). To begin properly, the philosopher must become once again an ordinary human being who lives, enjoys, undergoes, suffers, imagines, hopes, struggles, loves, and plans for the future. On this level, "experience" weaves together the environment, memory, reactions to physical conditions, interests, limitations, and projects envisioned. The opposition of "objective" conditions to "subjective" feeling has no place in such a scheme. Ordinary experience is woven together from multiple strands that do not assume the opposition of "subject" to "object."

The term "experience," Dewey argues, should be thought of as analogous to "life" or "history," words that blur the sharp boundaries between subjective and objective. "Life" requires the interpenetration of organism and environment. Reflective analysis can isolate the external conditions (air breathed, food taken) from internal ones (lungs breathing and stomach digesting), but such an isolation is the product of abstractive analysis not the concrete condition of actual living. Similarly, "history" is at the same time deeds, triumphs, and tragedies as well as the human retelling and interpretation of those acts (LW 1:19). The two dimensions can be separated in reflective abstraction, as can the alphabet from spoken language. But it must not be thought that the letters of the alphabet are original givens that are then put together synthetically. The original context is best represented by the experiences of ordinary persons. This context, as with the parallel cases of life and history, is one of undifferentiated, multilayered interpenetration.

Genuine empirical method, Dewey insists, "is the only method which can do justice to this inclusive integrity of 'experience.' It alone takes this integrated unity as the starting point for philosophic thought" (LW 1:19). Philosophical activity is a sort of circuit which begins in lived experience and must return there for both application and verification. The special service rendered by the study of philosophy is not, Dewey claims, the study of philosophy itself, but "a study, by means of philosophy, of life-experience" (LW 1:40).

Life-experience, as the example of Proust indicates, is multidimensional, complicated, laden with memory, emotion, and qualitative judgment. In the original first chapter of *Experience and Nature*, Dewey himself had reached into literature for examples of how "experience" should be understood. Rejecting the empiricist description of the chair, he offered these alternatives.

Consequently, I would rather take the behavior of the dog of Odysseus upon his master's return as an example of the sort of thing experience is for the philosopher than trust to such statements. A physiologist may for his special purpose reduce Othello's perception of a handkerchief to simple elements of color under certain conditions of light and shapes seen under certain angular conditions of vision. But the actual experience was charged with history and prophecy; full of love, jealousy and villainy, fulfilling past human relationships and moving fatally to tragic destiny. (LW 1:368)

The Galilean Purification is a prerequisite for taking the physiologist's description as paradigmatic. An inclusive empirical method must avoid the error of first simplifying and then reading the results of that simplification back as original data. Ordinary experience is something to be respected, not an illusion to be overcome. "The most serious indictment to be brought against non-empirical philosophies is that they have cast a cloud over the things of ordinary experience. They have not been content to rectify them. They have discredited them at large" (LW 1:40).

The public perception of philosophers as involved in arcane disputations, removed from the push and pull of ordinary life, disputations which disparage ordinary life-experience, may not be too far off the mark. Dewey wishes more than anything to reposition philosophy away from this overly specialized realm. He wants to return philosophy to its Socratic roots, where its efforts would revolve around the concerns and questions shared by both ordinary citizens and professional thinkers. "If what is written in these pages has no other result than creating and promoting a respect for concrete human experience and its potentialities, I shall be content" (LW 1:40–41).

The Fallacy of Intellectualism

Dewey has a name for the error committed by those who embrace a truncated empiricism. He calls it the "fallacy of intellectualism." "Intellectualism" is defined by Dewey as the view that "all experiencing is a mode of knowing, and that all subject-matter, all nature, is, in principle, to be reduced and transformed till it is defined in terms identical with the characteristics presented by refined objects of science as such" (LW 1:28).

Two starting points are possible. The correct path is the one which embraces everyday experience. The other believes that "all experiencing is a mode of knowing." It feels compelled to substitute "knowing," the results of intellectual inquiry, for the givens of ordinary experience. What we come to know as the result of specialized inquiries, that table salt is NaCl for example, should not be substituted for the ordinary experience of salt in all of its dimensions. Experiencing is always wider than knowing. The fallacy of intellectualism has been committed when the rich complexity of nature has been reduced to what a single type of inquiry has to say about it.

Dewey does not use the label "intellectualism" because he embraces some form of irrationalism. He is not deprecating the work of intelligence. He seeks to indicate, rather, the attitude which fails to recognize the primacy of lived experience. It substitutes the refined products of necessarily selective, often eliminative, cognition for the full richness of ordinary experience. By making this substitution it loses an opportunity to expand and enrichen our experience. Indeed, it narrows the province of philosophy. "Nature," as he put in the above citation, becomes "transformed" until it is thought of only in terms provided by specialized sciences.

This has led, historically, to the most prominent consequence flowing from "intellectualism": the artificial opposition of philosophy to science. If both disciplines are thought to share the same starting points, and to aim at the same goal, the differences in their results can only be interpreted as conflicting, not complementary, claims about the life-world. Philosophers, lovers of sweeping statements that they are, phrase this as the opposition of "appearance" to "reality."

A classic case of such a false dilemma was described by the physicist Arthur Eddington in his discussion of the "two tables." One was the commonsense table of ordinary experience. It was smooth, hard, colored, and had sharp edges. The other was the table described by a physicist. This one was mostly empty space, constantly in motion, with a small mass, and no clearly defined boundaries. Because he began by assuming that the *results* of a refined process of cognition, physics in this case, should be granted more existential stature, he concluded that the two perspectives were rivals. When forced to choose between them, he did not hesitate: "I need not tell you that modern physics has by delicate test and remorseless logic assured me that my second scientific table is the only one which is really there—wherever 'there' may be" (Eddington, xii).

The "remorseless logic" of which Eddington spoke was not, as he thought, that of physics. It was rather that of philosophy. Specifically it was, rather than "logic," a prior philosophical commitment to both the Galilean Purification and the Plotinian

Temptation. Such prior commitments, assuming that only a single view of reality can be determinative, and selecting the results of a particular inquiry rather than the givens of lived experience as that single view, lead inexorably to positions like those articulated by Eddington: different perspectives are competitors in the quest for the one true depiction of reality.

The best response to intellectualism begins with a rejection of the third faulty presupposition of traditional philosophy, the Asomatic Attitude. Humans are not primarily disembodied sorts of cogitators. They are embodied individuals, participants in multifarious sorts of interactions within the world that encompasses them. Reflective thought, using special methodologies, and exercised for specific purposes, can isolate various dimensions of that original transactional nexus. So long as it is kept in mind that these isolated elements have been selected for purposes of analysis, understanding, or control, no fallacy is committed. Such a procedure reflects embodied intelligence in action, not "intellectualism." Only when it is assumed that the products of cognitive reflection have ontological priority does intelligence in action degenerate into intellectualism. Only then would Eddington's two tables seem opposed to one another.

The Primacy of Interaction

The empirical method, as Dewey understands it, will reveal to us a world quite different from that presented by previous thinkers. One manner in which the Plotinian Temptation had manifested itself was by identifying separate, self-sufficient units as the ultimately real components of reality. Descartes had defined a "substance" as "a thing which exists in such a way as to depend on no other thing for its existence" (Descartes, 1985, 210). The most fully real things were thought to be independent unities. The more self-sufficient, the more autonomous was an entity, the more it approximated the ideal of full reality. Independent units of all sorts, from pure sense data, to unsplittable atoms, to the autonomous individuals which populated Locke's and Rousseau's states of nature, began to proliferate in philosophical and scientific literature.

So long as the soil within which philosophy germinated was that which had felt the prior working of the Galilean Purification and the Plotinian Temptation, such an emphasis on isolated units was understandable. But with the more fully human empiricism described by Dewey, the garden could be seen not as the space within which isolated entities could be found, but rather as a network of interconnections.

The crops are rooted *in* the soil, which is aerated *by* earthworms. Insects provide the means of pollination *for* the plants. Rain falls *on* them, and energy is received *from* the sun. The interconnections are real, even though traditional philosophers had failed to give them their due. William James was an important exception. He had already prepared the way by emphasizing the importance of conjunctions and prepositions in our descriptions of experience. "We ought to say a feeling of *and*, a feeling of *if*, a feeling of *but*, and a feeling of *by*, quite as readily as we say a feeling of *blue* and a feeling of *cold*" (James, 1950, 245–46).

Following James, Dewey suggests that a genuinely inclusive empirical method does not uncover isolated, discrete entities. Ordinary experience reveals entities in varied, multifarious forms of interrelationships. As Descartes himself quickly realized, only a divinity could live up to his definition of substance (Descartes, 1985, 210). So powerful was the Plotinian Temptation, however, that the belief in ultimately isolated units continued to be directive ideals, guiding philosophical reflection for several centuries.

Dewey does not succumb to the Plotinian Temptation because he does not make the coordinate commitment to the Galilean Purification. He feels under no compulsion to turn his back on human experiencing in order to begin with the artificially simplified world of entities in isolation. Dewey simply admits what lived experience prehends, the primacy of entities-in-interaction. His is an ecological stance in the sense that it grasps the reality and importance of interconnectedness. What we directly experience are spheres of interpenetration, conjunctions, reciprocating influences. Isolated entities are *not* raw givens of experience any more than were the sense data of Russell. They are "takens," aspects of experience highlighted for specific purposes. They are the refined products of abstractive mental processes. As such they are unproblematic. They become problematic only when they are claimed to have existential priority and offer a rival to our everyday, ordinary experience. Only then is there a fallacy of intellectualism.

Philosophy's task in part is to provide maps or charts of life-experience. This is the work of that branch of philosophy known as "metaphysics." Its task, as Dewey puts it, is to provide a "ground-map for the province of criticism" (LW 1:309). By "crit-

icism" Dewey means the process of evaluation. For such evaluation, "criticism," to occur fruitfully in areas such as art, political
organization, science, or social relations, the ground-map has
to be as carefully articulated as possible.

Traditional philosophers have referred to "being" as that
which is charted, described in metaphysics. Dewey employs
alternative formulations. He speaks of the "original material"
(LW 1:20) or the "affairs of every-day primary experience" (LW
1:36). Science, following the Galilean Purification, can work to
pare down the "affairs of every-day primary experience" in order
to achieve its aims. Without such a paring away, laboratories
would be useless. But philosophy, whose primary concern "is to
clarify, liberate and extend the goods which inhere in the naturally generated functions of experience" (LW 1:305), must
work always within the milieu of "every-day primary experience."

The novelty and radicality of Dewey's position will be over-
looked unless we keep firmly in mind that this original material,
directly experienced, can best be expressed as entities-in-interaction. The importance of this point for properly understanding
Dewey cannot be overemphasized. Interconnection and inter-
dependency are the rule. Isolated entities are mental constructions. They are products of selective emphasis.

Temporality and Possibility

Until Hegel, modern philosophy had relegated temporality to
an area of benign neglect. Two twentieth-century thinkers,
Bergson and Heidegger, took up the Hegelian lead and made
time central to their philosophies. Dewey, too, joins these
thinkers in returning time to a place of prominence. He is led to
this by his emphasis, also Hegelian, on the interrelatedness of
things. A world of entities-in-interaction is a world in which time
matters. Such a world is one in which the static terms "thing,"
"subject," and "object" do not capture the fullness of direct experience. Indeed, their very prominence results from minimizing
both the preposition-conjunctional dimension highlighted by
James, and the temporal dimension within which interrelations
take place.

In place of terms with static connotations, Dewey prefers the
word "affairs." "Nature," he claims, "is an affair *of* affairs." The
awareness that nature is a "scene of incessant beginnings and

endings, presents itself as the source of philosophic enlightenment" (LW 1:83).

Philosophic enlightenment derives from the awareness of temporality as a concrete presence, not just the "formal *a priori* condition of all our appearances whatsoever" that it was for Kant (Kant, 77). Indeed, it is better to speak of temporality as a quality of experience than to speak of "time" as an autonomous reality apart from the push and pull of natural processes. "Time as empty does not exist; time as an entity does not exist. What exists are things acting and changing, and a constant quality of their behavior is temporal" (LW 10:214). Wherever there is life-activity, entities-in-interaction, there are "affairs," literally "makings." "Affairs" are always in process and these processes, as temporal, lead to growth, change, and development.

A proper appreciation for temporality can only arise when the Asomatic Attitude is overcome. Awareness of the embodied character of human life allows us to appreciate how time is an integral character of experience. Philosophies which begin by assuming a bifurcated human nature can complain that the body is "trapped" in time. They can then seek an escape to an atemporal realm of eternal truths for mind. Dewey's empirical naturalism, by contrast, has no wish to escape from time. It welcomes temporality as an opportunity for growth.

The "affair" which is the individual human life, immersed as it is in temporality, does not have a fixed terminus at which point it can claim to be a completed or finished self. Vital temporality means that the affair which is our life is never completed. There can always be more development, more to learn, change of old habits, and cultivation of new ones. For Dewey, this continual process of development and awareness is summarized by the term "growth."[2] Since all entities are entities-in-process, they are continually being influenced and altered by the relationships in which they are immersed. The various projects we undertake, relationships into which we enter, and struggles which we undergo, help shape who we are.

When process and change are taken seriously, the affair that is a human being can be understood as a continuously growing self.

> Every event as such is passing into other things, in such a way that a later occurrence is an integral part of the *character* or *nature* of present existence. An "affair," *Res*, is

always at issue whether it concerns chemical change, the emergence of life, language, mind or the episodes that compose human history. (LW 1:92)

"Affairs" are never frozen, finished, or complete. They form a world characterized by genuine contingency and continual process. A world of affairs is a world of actualities open to a variety of possibilities.

"Thing," "subject," and "object" may connote entities as complete and finished, but "affair" indicates a process of making. The process of making, in turn, presupposes "possibility," an important corollary of temporality. Where temporality is taken seriously, possibility is elevated to a central category of existence. Indeed, possibility is a theme that plays a focal role in every aspect of Dewey's philosophy. Possibility is a *sine qua non* for knowing and evaluating, as well as the projects undertaken as a result of them. The possible, as that which, though not presently actual, may be brought into existence, bridges the gap between "ideas" and "ideals."

> From the standpoint of operational definition—of thinking in terms of action—the ideal and the possible are equivalent ideas. Idea and ideal have more in common than certain letters of the alphabet. Everywhere an idea, in its intellectual content, is a projection of what something existing may come to be. (LW 4:239)

Since Dewey rejects the Asomatic Attitude, it is not surprising that he makes no rigid separation between thought and action, or knowledge and value. Disembodied mental spectators may consider their role to be the detached contemplation of eternal ideals. For Dewey, such an interpretation falsifies how embodied intelligence actually works. Ideas and ideals are proleptic, anticipatory in function. Both involve possibilities.

Knowledge is the awareness of what something is. This, in turn, means a sensitivity to its multiple possibilities. To know something is to be aware of what might happen to it, what behavior to expect, what results will follow, what expectations to assume, under specified conditions. Maple syrup processors know what will happen to the sap under various environmental conditions. They know what an early thaw means, what warmer than typical nights mean for the flow of sap. The burgeoning of our knowledge grows proportionately with our ability to anticipate what possibilities will be realized under various circumstances. It grows with new circumstances which reveal more about the natural process. Knowledge is not an affair of coming directly into the presence of the "really real" once and for all. Knowing is temporally conditioned. It grows with the varying circumstances as we become more sensitive to the possibilities that can be realized in the varying circumstances in which we and whatever it is we are trying to understand are placed.

The cognate notion of ideals involves the projection of possible conditions, different from the present, conditions which will preserve already attained goods and secure new ones. All moral, social, political reform begins with ideas, the suggestions of altered situations which, if brought into being, could improve our existential situation. The already existing, by that very fact, is excluded from the realm of the ideal. This latter is coextensive with possibilities for change.

Responsibility

A ground-map whose central markers are "affairs," "temporality," and "possibility," is one whose author would have a hard time evading the burden of responsibility. It admits that a variety of possibilities can always be realized. Careful reflection is first needed to determine which should become ends to be achieved, and which discouraged. Such reflection needs to be complemented by a concerted effort to transform the desired possibilities into actualities. A world of affairs is one in which activity, process, and contingency are interwoven. Progress is neither inevitable as the optimist would hold, nor hopeless as would hold the pessimist. A world where possibilities are ever-present is a world in which intelligent participants have to gauge carefully the consequences of their actions. It is a world in which their status as participants cannot be abrogated.

Some philosophers have followed a different path. Resignation to existing conditions and/or withdrawal from them have been prominent avenues of escape. Epicurus (341–270 B.C.), for example, preached the aim of achieving imperturbability by withdrawing from the active life to seek a happiness associated with peace of soul. Descartes, as part of the Hellenistic influenced stream of Modern philosophy, offered an analogous prescription.

My third maxim was always to try to conquer myself rather
than fortune, to change my desires rather than the order of
the world; and generally to become accustomed to believing
that there is nothing that is utterly within our power, except
for our thoughts, so that, after having done our best regarding things external to us, everything that fails to bring us
success, from our point of view, is absolutely impossible.
(Descartes, 1980, 14)

Acquiescence of this sort is absolutely foreign to Dewey. A
world of affairs is one of process, activity, and possibilities. Such
a world is not one in which responsibility is to be shunned. Larry
Hickman's book on Dewey ends with an epilogue, appropriately
titled, "Responsible Technology." He cites with approval E. A.
Burtt's comments at the centennial celebration of Dewey's birth
that "if he had to pick a single word to typify Dewey's philosophical work, it would be 'responsibility'" (Hickman, 196).[3] Burtt
and Hickman are correct to focus on this term. For Dewey,
humans are participants in a world of ongoing, interwoven, contingent affairs. It is incumbent upon them to act in such a way
that will encourage the realization of those possibilities appropriate to flourishing sociopolitical life. Such a life can be realized
in no other way.

Because his philosophy is rooted in everyday, ordinary
experience, sociopolitical concerns are always paramount for
Dewey. He admitted in his autobiography that these issues took
on for him an importance usually reserved in others for religious
concerns (LW 5:154). We can now see why this sort of religious
devotion to moral and social issues was no arbitrary choice. The
whole orientation of empirical naturalism culminates quite rea-
sonably in the challenge of responsible involvement: the call to
participate in channelling the energies of our surrounding world
in such a way as to preserve and enhance the goods we already
have, while attempting to secure new ones.

Dewey thus distinguishes himself at a stroke from his
younger contemporaries, Martin Heidegger (1889–1976), Ludwig
Wittgenstein (1889–1951), and Alfred North Whitehead
(1861–1947). Each of these thinkers held strong beliefs and cared
deeply about social goods. None of them, however, articulated a
detailed sociopolitical philosophy consistent with their overall
outlook. Dewey, on the other hand, wrote copiously on political

philosophy. These writings, supporting a specific form of democracy, were fully in line with his belief that "in some sense all philosophy is a branch of morals" (LW 1:387).[4]

Evaluating Philosophy

Given the whole orientation of empirical naturalism, it is not surprising that Dewey's criterion for a successful philosophy is to be found in the social and cultural realm of lived experience. The challenge of securing and extending goods is the real test of a philosophy. It is not to be judged primarily by its logical rigor, secure apodictic foundations, success at interpreting the discoveries of science, or the manner in which it identifies the primary causes of existence. The real sign of a vibrant philosophy is its fruitfulness in guiding us toward enhanced human lives. When we want to judge a philosophy, its role in providing the conditions for a flourishing life are paramount.

> Does it (philosophy) end in conclusions which, when they are referred back to ordinary life-experiences and their predicaments, render them more significant, more luminous to us, and make our dealings with them more fruitful? Or does it terminate in rendering the things of ordinary experience more opaque than they were before? . . . Does it yield the enrichment and increase of power of ordinary things which the results of physical science afford when applied in every-day affairs? Or does it become a mystery that these ordinary things should be as they are; and are philosophic concepts left to dwell in separation in some technical realm of their own. (LW 1:18)

Professional philosophy fails this Deweyan test miserably. So much of it dwells in the separate, technical realm disparaged in this quotation. Not only is it remote from daily life, but it too often construes itself as a rival to it. "The things of ordinary experience," as Dewey expresses it, become more "opaque than ever before." Socrates is the great model philosopher for Dewey, someone fully immersed in the concerns of living a good life. Philosophy, ultimately, is the quest to secure and enlarge what is good in life. Its task is to render "more significant" our "ordinary life experiences," and to make "more fruitful" our dealings with them.

Modernity's futile quest for certainty has resulted in a factitious bifurcation between that world and the "really real." The
rivalry thus established is what leads "cultivated common sense
to look askance at philosophy" (LW 1:187). It also allows philosophers to abdicate what empirical naturalism embraces, the
responsibility for dealing with important substantive issues.

Nicholas Rescher has speculated about what would happen were philosophy to lose its niche as a well-established field
within the world of higher education. One important ramification
would occur in the area of publishing. "Textbooks would vanish.
Journaldom would collapse. All those articles anthologies would
vanish from the face of the earth." In their place, a new sort of
philosophical writing would emerge. It would not be one aimed at
colleagues or "graduate students seen as prospective colleagues."
"One could no longer presuppose knowledge of technicalities or
interest in esoterica. One would have to write on basic issues and
to do so clearly and interestingly—in a way accessible to readers
at large." Such a vision, so removed from the present philosophical climate, did not frighten Rescher. "What a difference! And—
come to think of it—one that doesn't sound all that terrible"
(Rescher, 355). Had Deweyan empirical naturalism remained a
force in American philosophy, no such exhortation would have
been necessary.

2

Thinking

Against Epistemology

The detective story, according to Umberto Eco, is the most philosophical of literary genres (Eco, 1984, 53–54). Because the crime disturbs the social equilibrium, it occasions questioning, reflection, and conjecture. As a corollary to Eco's comments I would add that the evolution of detective literature parallels changes in philosophical perspectives. The first detective in fiction, Poe's C. Auguste Dupin, was comfortable with the Asomatic Attitude. Reflection, for Dupin, could best be accomplished by withdrawing into a darkened room. "'If it is any point requiring reflection,' observed Dupin, as he forbore to enkindle the wick, 'we shall examine it to better purpose in the dark'" (Poe, 226).In Dupin's world, thinking is an inner process, one that can best be pursued in isolation from the body and its distractions.

Eco's own *In the Name of the Rose* introduces a different sort of detective. Friar William is no deductive machine. The crime cannot be solved simply by adding together all of the facts and retiring to a quiet place for deducing the solution. There are, to begin with, too many facts. The pivotal ones do not come with labels indicating their importance. Determining which ones are relevant and which ones are peripheral is the first task of the detective. But this, in turn, cannot be done adequately without tentative hypotheses which help organize the multiplicity of data. The imaginative projection of hypotheses and the collection of data are correlative. They cannot go on independently of one another.

Friar William is tentative, proposing various conjectures, following out their consequences. Retiring to a darkened room for undisturbed cogitation is not sufficient. The objective can only be attained if multiple possibilities are imagined. Such a procedure is frustrating to Friar William's young assistant, Adso, who has textbook notions of philosophy, knowledge, and truth. His master's method, he says,

> seemed to me quite alien to that of the philosopher, who reasons by first principles, so that his intellect almost assumes the ways of the divine intellect. I understand that, when he didn't have an answer, William proposed many to himself, very different from one another. . . . I had the impression that William was not at all interested in the truth, which is nothing but the adjustment between the thing and the intellect. On the contrary, he amused himself by imagining how many possibilities were possible. (Eco, 1983, 367–68)

The elements that Adso assumes will be present, a God-like disembodied mind, knowledge resulting from the mind's direct contact with the object, and a reason working apart from imagination, are just those elements which Dewey seeks to banish from his own articulation of thinking. For him, thinking is a human, not a merely mental, activity. Imagination plays an important role in projecting possibilities. Hands-on bodily involvement in the form of experimentation is crucial to resolving problematic situations.

Empirical naturalism involves a move in the direction of Friar William and away from Dupin. It revises traditional beliefs about the processes of thinking and knowing. Dewey calls this reconstructed interpretation "an empirical theory of ideas." He signals its importance by praising it as "one of the three or four outstanding feats of intellectual history" (LW 4:92). It is such a significant feat because it undermines the Modern approach to knowledge. This approach was encapsulated in the term "epistemology," a term Dewey almost always uses derisively.

Epistemology flourished in special circumstances of time and place, the Modern period (1600–1900) in Europe. During this time, it came more and more to be considered the central philosophical discipline. So closely intertwined were philosophy and epistemology that as late as 1912 Bertrand Russell could write a book devoted mainly to epistemological issues and entitle it *The Problems of Philosophy*.

Epistemology's roots are found in the dualisms of mind and body, of subject and object that have dominated modernity.

Within this dualistic framework, the interiority of the "subject" came to have a life of its own, separate from what was more and more referred to as the "external" world.[1] Such a bifurcated context accounts for some defining characteristics which Dewey associated with epistemology:

1. It asks certain sorts of factitious questions, for example, whether knowledge of the external world is possible.
2. It offers narrow alternatives for the positions that can resolve its problems. These positions typically take an either/or form, and have been manifested as the dilemmas of idealism *or* realism, rationalism *or* empiricism, absolutism *or* relativism.
3. Epistemology leads to unending puzzlement about ordinary experience.[2]

Dewey's opposition to "epistemology" is not a refusal to treat seriously the questions relating to knowledge. It is more an attempt to recover a pre-Modern way of addressing such questions. "In Greek thought," says Dewey, epistemology "as distinct from logic and psychology, can hardly be said to have existed" (MW 6:440). Like Plato, Dewey does address questions of thinking and knowing, but always within the wider context of social and moral issues, which are *the* central philosophical concerns.

In addition, empirical naturalism allows Dewey to treat thinking and knowing in a different manner than the way they are investigated in epistemology. His revised interpretation is an outgrowth of the central notions of empirical naturalism discussed in the previous chapter: an ontology of entities-in-interaction, the rejection of intellectualism, the pervasive importance of temporality, and the central role of possibility.

One problem with Dewey's novel attitude is that he christened it with the misleading names "instrumentalism" and "pragmatism."[3] The first seemed to suggest that Dewey was not concerned about the truth of how things are. The second was a label often thought to mean simply "if it works, then it's true." Dewey tried to disassociate his use of these terms from unwelcome connotations, but was generally unsuccessful. The most accurate label he provided for the revised position was the expression "intelligence in operation" (LW 4:163). Just how this "intelligence in operation" is characterized and what is its relation to philosophy will be the topics taken up in this chapter.

Copernican Revolutions

With regard to questions of knowledge, there are two philosophers who believed that their redirections of thought had accomplished a feat as significant as that of Copernicus. Both invoked the name of the Polish astronomer. Yet the contrast between the two Copernican Revolutions in philosophy could not have been greater. The first was articulated in Immanuel Kant's *Critique of Pure Reason* (1781), the second in Dewey's *The Quest for Certainty* (1929).

Kant was a philosopher rooted in Modern, post-Cartesian assumptions. His focal concerns were epistemological. He continued, in the terms of Dewey's title, the Cartesian quest for certainty. Kant went so far as to introduce a Greek word which would indicate the degree to which he sought necessary and absolute truth: *apodicticity*. His Copernican Revolution grew out of the awareness, forcefully expressed by Hume, that apodicticity remained impossible as long as cognition was dependent upon experience of objects. Quite properly, Kant was troubled by what this meant for the foundations of Newtonian science and Euclidean geometry. To salvage these latter, he assumed that in addition to the *a posteriori* sort of knowledge embraced by the empiricists, there must also be *a priori* conditions of knowledge. These conditions, not at all dependent upon experience, are what Kant believed were necessary to answer the troubling implications of Humean skepticism.

This philosophical reformation involved the abandonment of an object-centered epistemology in favor of a subject-centered one. Kant saw this as marking so major a shift that he was willing to compare it to the reorientation occasioned by Copernicus. "We must therefore make a trial whether we may not have more success in the tasks of metaphysics, if we suppose that objects must conform to our knowledge. . . . We should then be proceeding precisely on the lines of Copernicus' primary hypothesis" (Kant, 22). By attempting as daring and as counterintuitive a transposition in philosophy as Copernicus had attempted in astronomy, Kant sought to set firmly in place the foundations for apodicticity.

From a Deweyan perspective, Kant's attempt to recapture certainty for philosophy is (1) misguided, and (2) actually a Ptolemaic rather than a Copernican strategy. As someone wholly implicated in the world of ordinary experience, Dewey is wary of philosophical strategies that try to downplay or deny outright the precarious and tentative character of human experience. The title of Dewey's book, *The Quest for Certainty*, highlights a prominent but mistaken impetus that dominated Modern philosophy. This quest has led, as in Kant, to the constitution of artificial, unverifiable apparati which are needed as foundations for apodicticity. Dewey puts into question not only the results of this quest, but the motivations that brought it into being.

A philosopher rooted in ordinary experience accepts the combined existential package of contingency, responsibility, and the possibility of failure. Peril, resulting from the fragility and fallibility of our condition, is an unavoidable accompaniment of that condition. Modernity, however, dominated as it was by the Galilean Purification's attempt to stand outside the human condition, engaged in a quest for certainty. This quest was motivated by the desire, as Dewey put it in the title of his first chapter, to "escape from peril."

> The quest for certainty is a quest for a peace which is assured, an object which is unqualified by risk and the shadow of fear which action casts. For it is not uncertainty *per se* which men dislike, but the fact that uncertainty involves us in peril of evils. (LW 4:7)

Dewey is no philosopher of escape. Like the young Heidegger, who complained that instead of seeking the easy way out, philosophers should set for themselves the task of restoring existence to its original difficulty (Caputo, 1), Dewey rejects all escapist philosophies. As we saw in the previous chapter, philosophers are also ordinary human beings immersed in lived experience. Because their task involves securing and expanding real goods in this world, they must root themselves in it, not in an artificial construction which must be projected if the hubristic aim of apodicticity is to be achieved.

In addition to the claim that it was misguided, Dewey argued that Kant's was really a Ptolemaic revolution. Within the Kantian position, human cognition is reestablished as a fixed center about which all else revolves (LW 4:229). By suggesting *a priori* conditions that are atemporal and acontextual, Kant, despite his intentions, actually moved philosophy backward.

There is one dimension in the Kantian analysis, however, which remains important for Dewey's own Copernican

Revolution. This is Kant's emphasis on human understanding as active and not merely passive. Aristotle had first suggested what came to be known in Scholasticism as the "active" or "agent" intellect. This was the Aristotelian tradition's way of indicating that the human intellect did not simply receive data, but acted on them in an original and constructive manner. Within British empiricism, the medieval agent intellect had been attenuated until its activity was defined as merely the permutation and combination of the simple givens of experience.

Kant's reintroduction of a genuinely active, originative capacity for intelligence was a badly needed corrective. Unfortunately, Kant's reaction was an overreaction. He gave too much power to a human intelligence conceived as overly isolated from its natural context. Nonetheless, if Kant's claim that "receptivity can make knowledge possible only when combined with spontaneity" (Kant, 130), is set within a Deweyan interactive, embodied context, it indicates the contours of the latter's Copernican Revolution. The heart of this revolution involved the central Deweyan theme of interaction.

> The new centre is indefinite interactions taking place within a course of nature which is not fixed and complete, but which is capable of direction to new and different results through the mediation of intentional operations. Neither self nor world, neither soul nor nature (in the sense of something isolated and finished in isolation) is the centre, any more than either earth or sun is the absolute centre of a single universal and necessary frame of reference. (LW 4:232)

In addition to the emphasis on interaction, this citation also admits the embodied nature of human life by its stress on the "mediation of intentional operations." Knowledge does not arise from mere reflection. Knowing cannot be separated from doing. To understand subject-matters ever more fully, operations must be undertaken which allow the many dimensions of subject-matters to manifest themselves.

In the end, we have to admit that Dewey's revolution named after Copernicus was more radical than even that of the astronomer. As popularly understood, Copernicus had substituted one center for another. Empirical naturalism disallows any absolute centers. It admits that the component elements of a situation reciprocally influence each other.

Spectators or Inquirers?

A world of interacting, mutually influencing affairs does not readily lend itself to the metaphor for knowing which dominated modernity, that of sight. The hegemony of "epistemology" was accompanied by an association of knowledge with vision.[4] The "subject" had a cognitive task, which was to perceive the "objects" which existed in the external world. The model knower on this scheme was a detached "spectator" simply enumerating the data received:

> The theory of knowing is modeled after what was supposed to take place in the act of vision. The object refracts light to the eye and is seen; it makes a difference to the eye and to the person having an optical apparatus, but none to the thing seen. The real object is the object so fixed in its regal aloofness that it is a king to any beholding mind that may gaze upon it. A spectator theory of knowledge is the inevitable outcome. (LW 4:19)

The ideal knower, on the traditional scheme, was imagined as someone looking on disinterestedly from behind a plate-glass window. The data from the objects could then be taken in with minimal subjective interference. If there were problems with knowing, the fault was thought to rest with the distorting optical apparatus. It had to be polished and thereby improved. To this end, Francis Bacon identified four "idols" as standard distorting factors which had to be removed prior to the direct and correct apprehension of data (Bacon, aphorisms 39–65).

The process of knowing, on this spectator view, was like the children's game of "hidden pictures." The artefacts, animals, plants, and people to be espied were already in the picture. No changes needed be made in the data. What was needed was a more concerted effort on the part of the viewer, until the appropriate data came into focus. Such a knowing situation was bipolar. There was a *subject*, the spectator-knower, confronting an *object*, that which was to be known. The spectator-knower's primary task was to gather information until a particular result was attained, the adjustment, as Adso put it, "between the thing and the intellect."

Deweyan philosophy alters this paradigm significantly. In the life-world dominated by interactions, the older terminological uses of "subject" and "object" are simply not applicable. The "subjects" are no longer the humans endowed with inner consciousness whose main relation to the world is that of spectators. Returning to what he considers to be a pre-Modern usage, Dewey, long before French philosophers made the death of the "subject" popular, identified, not the cogitating self, but the affairs of the world as "subjects." They are subject-matters to be investigated.[5] The "objects" are the objectives aimed at in such investigations.[6] Humans are "inquirers" who, as a result of some interest, are examining the subject-matters in light of a particular objective.[7]

Instead of the bipolar knowing situation envisioned by Modern epistemology, we now have a tridimensional paradigm: inquirer, subject-matter, and objective. Scientists, in their approach to problems are exemplary in this regard. They do not consider themselves to be mere spectators. They are interested individuals seeking more information about the subject-matters that make up the context within which they are immersed. By referring to the material-under-investigation as subject-matter rather than as "object," Dewey deflects the Plotinian temptation to fasten onto *one* meaning as ultimately determinative. Subject-matters can be investigated from various perspectives, depending on the "objective" of inquiry. The primacy of any particular set of results can only be judged in relation to the purposes of inquiry. It is not a direct intuition of the single, "really real" structure hidden behind appearances.

On the bipolar model, for example, the human "subjects" trying to understand the "object" water may be said to have completed their task once the chemical composition H_2O has been identified. As Descartes put it in his *Discourse*, "since there is only one truth concerning any matter, whoever discovers this truth knows as much as can be known" (Descartes, 121). It is less likely, on the Deweyan model, that subject-matter will be confused with a unidimensional "object" to be attained once and for all. The term "subject-matter" encourages both respect for the multifarious character of affairs, and for the varied perspectives from which they can be examined.

When water is understood as a subject-matter, and not an object, certain new emphases are introduced. Whereas the bipolar view reinforces the Plotinian Temptation for unity, the triadic understanding allows for multiple investigations. A community may wish to inquire as to whether water from a certain source is potable or not. They may wish to identify the mineral content in their water. Others may wish to examine the role of water in the history of human communities. Some may want to examine the symbolic uses of water in religious practices, while others may be interested in the role water plays in the healthy development of crops. The subject-matters that surround us, like water, are not one-dimensional objects waiting to be viewed correctly once and for all. They are subject-matters, repositories of multiple possibilities, many of which remain latent until the activities of inquirers help bring them out.

Articulating the knowing situation in terms of *inquirers*, *sub-ject-matters*, and *objectives* brings with it another benefit. It minimizes the temptation to assume the Asomatic Attitude. The exemplaric instance of coming to know is not, for Dewey, the image of C. August Dupin reflecting in the dark, but that of an experimenter manipulating the subject-matter and introducing changes into it. The spectator can have perceived water and have reflected on it for a long time and still not come to realize its capacity for putting out fires. Nor, having once come to recognize this capacity, will the inquirer automatically come to know that some fires are actually aggravated by having water added to them.

Traditional epistemology tended to think on the model of "a spectator viewing a finished picture rather than after that of the artist producing a painting." This bipolar model was responsible for the "questions of epistemology with which the technical student of philosophy is so familiar, and which have made Modern philosophy in especial so remote from the understanding of the everyday person and from the results and processes of science."

"Epistemology" also helped drive a sharp wedge between the artist, whose imaginative constructions were thought to be fanciful and subjective, and the scientist, whose task was to espy reality as it really, objectively, was. Dewey's tridimensional model blurs such a sharp contrast. Thinking and knowing can best be understood by considering the activity of an artist or scientist experimenting with different materials.

> If knowing were habitually conceived of as active and operative, after the analogy of experiment guided by hypothesis, or of invention guided by the imagination of some possibility, it is not too much to say that the first effect would be to emancipate philosophy from all the epistemological puzzles which now perplex it. (MW 12: 150)[8]

Empirical naturalism realizes that we come to fuller comprehension by acting on subject-matters. If the eye and vision provided the guiding metaphors for "epistemology," it is the hands and manipulation that play this role for Deweyan intelligence in operation.

Epistemology addressed artificial problems about the very possibility of knowing because of its prior commitments to a bipolar subject/object description of existence. Dewey sought rather, as indicated by one of his titles, to describe *How We Think* (MW 6). The everyday experience of humans is one in which there are no hard and fast separations between thinking and doing. Inquiry is a participational, active form of human behavior. The real contrast with the older views, says Dewey, is that between a notion of experience that is "empirical" (he should have said "empiricist") and one that is "experimental" (LW 4:65).

Inquiry for traditional empiricists is inquiry modelled on a subject as spectator receiving data from the objective world. To label inquiry "experimental," by contrast, highlights the practice made prominent in the sciences that knowing results from processes that involve doing. Only by manipulating the subject-matters of inquiry, by subjecting them to various forms of combinations and interactions, can there be emergence of traits and properties that would have remained latent under different conditions. Examining water in isolation from multiple interactions would prevent its important property of inhibiting some fires from emerging. In order to arrive at that awareness, some activity, some altering of conditions, some experimentation, has to take place.

The importance of the Deweyan outlook which admits the "active and operative" character of inquiry, together with its temporal and spatial situatedness, is threefold.

1. The Plotinian Temptation to reduce knowing to a single, privileged perspective is undermined.
2. The importance of experimentation is affirmed.
3. Inquiry can be seen to aim at continual growth in awareness, not any once and for all direct confrontation with Being.

Don Quixote seemed a pathetically comic figure within the emerging epistemology of Modern Europe. Everywhere he saw multiple meanings, while the spirit of the age sought to identify the single, true meaning. His was a pre-Modern consciousness, out of place and therefore marginalized in the new soil of the Modern epoch.

The post-Modern soil prepared by Deweyan philosophy helps rehabilitate the man from La Mancha. The subject-matters of the world present multiple possibilities for meaning. They can be examined in light of many objectives. Don Quixote, vanquished by the forces of Modern epistemology, may find himself newly appreciated in a post-Deweyan world.

The Traits of Inquiry

Inquiry, with its triadic ingredients, can be described as including the following characteristics:

1. Doubt, uncertainty and puzzlement are not merely "subjective." It is situations themselves that are problematic, or questionable.
2. Inquiries involve a somatic intelligence in operation, that is to say, manipulation, some form of doing on the part of inquirers.
3. The procedures of inquiry are anti-reductionistic.
4. Responsibility is a human accompaniment of inquiry.

Problematic Situations

As we have already seen, empirical naturalism rejects the Galilean Purification with its atemporal, acontextual starting points. The qualitatively permeated world of ordinary experience is the matrix within which the method of intelligence begins its search for what Dewey calls "warranted assertions."[9] The life-world is one of complex affairs and situations. Within that world certain aspects present themselves as "unsettled" or "tensional." Antecedently established meanings do not suffice for resolving them. Resolutions can be accomplished only by transforming the unsettled elements into newly assured, smoothly fitting components in a newly stabilized situation.

"Problematic" aspects could involve a parent's concern about a child's reading habits, a physician's puzzlement about a patient's symptoms, a farmer's worry about increasingly acidic soil, or a paleontologist's questions about missing links in the fossil record. Whatever the particular concern, it is important to realize that it is the *situation* that is problematic. Such a view can best be understood if we recall the discussion of the previous chapter.

The natural world in its full, concrete sense is a sphere of overlapping, and criss-crossing affairs. Within the framework of the older empiricism, which substituted abstracted, artificially separated elements for the affairs of concrete actuality, it was possible to assert that "*we* are doubtful, puzzled, confused, undecided; *objects* are complete, assured, fixed" (LW 4:185). This represents the pre-Copernican view. An ontology of affairs, of entities-in-interaction, cannot revert to such an artificial sorting out of isolated subjects "over here," and an external world populated by objects "over there." Only in a world dominated by such separations was it possible to identify the uncertainty, indeterminacy, doubtfulness, wholly with the so-called "subject."

Dewey employs many terms to indicate the kind of situation within which questioning and a line of inquiry emerge: "disturbed, troubled, ambiguous, confused, full of conflicting tendencies, obscure." Whichever term he uses, he is careful to indicate that, in each case, an accurate description identifies the situation itself as occasioning inquiry.

> It is the *situation* that has these traits. *We* are doubtful because the situation is inherently doubtful. Personal states of doubt that are not evoked by and are not relative to some existential situation are pathological; when they are extreme they constitute the mania of doubting. Consequently, situations that are disturbed and troubled, confused or obscure, cannot be straightened out, cleared up and put in order, by manipulation of our personal states of mind. (LW 12:109–10)

There are no isolated entities in the Deweyan ontology. Genuine, specific doubts, not the fabricated absolute doubt of Descartes, continuously emerge from interactions. Certain conditions prevail in our surroundings and they evoke a response from us. The conditions apart from our presence are mere events, occurrences. Our presence defined as outsiders, unaffected by the context is a pre-Copernican fantasy. Only as we recognize our status as inevitably implicated in a world of affairs, will we be properly positioned to grasp the full import of unsettled, indeterminate situations.

Embodied Intelligence

Since doubt, uncertainty, and confusion are not merely internal, subjective, phenomena, the path of inquiry also cannot be merely mental or internal. As we have already seen, inquiries involve some doing, some active participation of individuals, which alters existing conditions with the aim of establishing a new level of harmonious integration. The parent concerned about a child's reading habits may want to consult with that child's teacher, set aside time for reading aloud, or modify the family's television habits. The physician will run a variety of tests, check data bases, seek advice from colleagues, prescribe medication for the patient. The farmer will consult experts, experiment with different ways of modifying the soil, plant alternative crops. The paleontologist will reexamine the fossil record, explore possible reasons for the discrepancies, place in question the theory that leads to specific expectations.

In each case an indeterminate situation is moved toward determinacy via somatic intelligence, that is to say, thoughtful manipulation. Experimentation is not haphazard. It is guided by ideas understood as hypothetical anticipations of desired results. Intelligence means "operations actually performed in the modification of conditions, including all the guidance that is given by means of ideas, both direct and symbolic" (LW 4:160).

This process defines the extent of Dewey's much misunderstood "instrumentalism." Admittedly, Dewey fastened onto an unfortunate label for his position. It made him sound Baconian in the sense that the natural world seemed to be valued simply as "raw material," as mere "instrumentality" to be bent in the direction of a narrow, expeditious human will. Dewey's own formulations may have provided some support for such an interpretation. He was reacting, after all, to the view that humans were simply passive onlookers to the spectacle of Being. But he did not, save in some unguarded rhetorical flourishes, overreact to the extent of denying intrinsic appreciation for the immediately felt qualities of things. Indeed, the world of immediate, ordinary experience is, as we have amply seen, the place where all reflection must begin.

"Instrumentalism" was a label meant to identify the function of ideas. They were, as hypothetical anticipations, to serve a mediating function in inquiry. Their role was to help bring an indeterminate situation to a new level of determinateness. This intermediate role is what allows the method of intelligence in operation to be characterized as "instrumental." Ideas are, in a favorite Deweyan term, "proleptic" (LW 12:122). They involve anticipated consequences. As such, they provide tentative suggestions for resolving problematic situations. Their mediating, "instrumental" status derives from the fact that the indeterminate situation is not made determinate simply by the generation of ideas. These must serve to direct the activities which strive to render the situation determinate or resolved. Ideas are not ends in themselves. They form an important part of a circuit that results in a new level of equilibrium.

> It is in this sense that all reflective knowledge as such is instrumental. The beginning and the end are things of gross everyday experience. But apart from knowledge the things of our ordinary experience are fragmentary, casual, unregulated by purpose, full of frustrations and barriers. In the language previously used, they are problematic, obstructive, challenges to thought. . . . Reflective knowledge is the *only* means of regulation. Its value as instrumental is unique. (LW 4:174–75)[10]

Such an understanding of instrumentalism does not in any way deny the intrinsic value of many inquiries. They may well be carried out as ends in themselves. The resolution of a particular problematic situation need not be instrumental to a further purpose. A father wants his child to be able to read, a physician wants to restore a patient to health. These are ends in themselves. They need not be subservient to further ends that serve either the parent or the physician.

The process of resolving these unsettled situations, however, will inevitably involve an instrumental phase. Intelligence "means operations actually performed in the modification of conditions, including all the guidance that is given by means of ideas, both direct and symbolic" (LW 4:160). The method of intelligence "marks a transitional redirection and rearrangement of the real. It is indeterminate and instrumental; it comes between a relatively casual and accidental experience of existence and one relatively settled and defined" (LW 4:236).

Anti-Reductionism

"Instrumentalism," properly understood, helps Dewey circumvent the problem of reductionism, the view that there is one, fundamental description of reality and that alternative descriptions, if they are to mirror the "really real," must be translated, or "reduced" to that fundamental one. Eddington's example of the two tables offers a classic case of reduction. The common sense description must be retranslated into the language of physics if we are to provide *the* objective description of what is "really" there. Empirical naturalism, however, does not accept the bipolar spectator stance which occasions the ideal of one, final description of reality. As a result, it does not succumb to the Plotinian Temptation toward unity.

The move from "epistemology" to "intelligence in operation" thus minimizes the tendency to posit Eddington-like rival realities. Subject-matters may be approached in many ways, in light of many objectives. There is, as Dewey points out, "no kind of inquiry which has a monopoly of the honorable title of knowledge. The engineer, the artist, the historian, the man of affairs attain knowledge in the degree they employ methods that enable them to solve problems which develop in the subject-matter they are concerned with" (LW 4:176).

Humans who face unsettled situations must attempt to resolve them by employing ideas and experimentations that are specific to their concerns. They need not aim at following procedures identical with those of a particular, privileged science, say physics. "Intelligence in operation" helps to overcome the prejudice that grants a hegemony to one limited field of inquiry.

> All materials of experience are equally real; that is, all are existential; each has a right to be dealt with in terms of its own especial characteristics and its own problems. To use philosophical terminology, each type of subject-matter is entitled to its own characteristic categories, according to the questions it raises and the operations necessary to answer them. (LW 4:172)

There is no single methodology applicable to every area of human concern. Inquiries do share the generic traits that have been identified: they have a triadic structure, they begin with a genuinely problematic situation, and they can come to a resolution via processes of manipulation and experimentation. But this pattern allows great latitude for specific methodologies which must be coordinated with the types of problematic situations needing to be resolved. There is no final, foundational language to which all the others must be reduced.

Succumbing to the Plotinian Temptation by imposing *one* hegemonic standard of investigation and accuracy makes little sense in a world so rich and diverse as ours.

> In fact, the painter may know colors as well as the physicist; the poet may know stars, rain and clouds as well as the meteorologist; the statesman, educator and dramatist may know human nature as truly as the professional psychologist; the farmer may know soils and plants as truly as the botanist and the mineralogist. (LW 4:176)

There are many kinds of indeterminate situations and each requires special sorts of criteria in order to bring about a new equilibrium. Empirical naturalism incorporates the generous attitude that knowledge flourishes in many fields. "There are as many conceptions of knowledge as there are distinctive operations by which problematic situations are resolved" (LW 4:176–77).

Responsibility

The generosity of empirical naturalism, together with the instrumental character of ideas, means that the burden of responsibility, so central to the Deweyan undertaking, can only be avoided by willful blindness. Inquirers cannot easily retreat from the world of ordinary experience, nor hide behind the claim that their concerns are merely "intellectual" or "theoretical." "The change," says Dewey, "from an intrinsic rationality in the traditional sense to an intelligibility to be realized by human action places responsibility upon human beings" (LW 4:172).

A participatory intelligence in operation identifies thinking as part of a circuit which always returns to ordinary experience. Embodied intelligence involves modification of conditions. Because these modifications may bring along with them consequences for good or ill, they involve the inquirer in a web of responsibility.

Utopia is, as its etymology suggests, "no place." Wherever we find existence we also find limitations, weaknesses, evils. Any situation can be improved. One sort of problematic dimension which permeates all of human existence is the challenge to secure, enhance, and increase goods. The circuit of activity which involves reflection requires a return to the context of weal and woe which characterizes the world of everyday, lived experience. Responsibility is incorporated into "pragmatic instrumentalism" which considers "*both* knowledge and practice as means of making goods—excellencies of all kinds—secure in experienced existence" (LW 4:30).

The Role of Philosophy

"Making goods secure" also identifies the wider task of philosophy. The life-world is neither a neutral context of mere facts, nor a realm of fixed values antecedently determined and universally binding. It is a world which combines immediate satisfactions, strivings, benumbing "everydayness" (to borrow an apt Heideggerian coinage), frustrations, and fulfillments. Since ours is an attempt to live as temporal creatures who have some say in determining the conditions which surround us, lived experience is inherently and unavoidably moral.

Our constant and unescapable concern is with prosperity and adversity, success and failure, achievement and frustration, good and bad. Since we are all creatures with lives to live, and find ourselves within an uncertain environment, we are constructed to note and judge in terms of bearing upon weal and woe—upon value. (LW 1:33)

Philosophy's place is within this matrix of weal and woe. Too often, as we saw in the preceding chapter, philosophy has served as an avenue of escape, a route of solace and detachment from the pressing complicated difficulties of life. This is the false path of ivory tower philosophers. Dewey's Copernican Revolution involves so marked a shift in orientation that the tendency to escapism is minimized. Thinking, doing, and responsibility, as we have seen, are continuous and intertwined.

The Modern project in philosophy with its roots in dualism and its emphasis on epistemology, encouraged the kind of escape Dewey sought to overcome. Philosophy could then view itself as a self-contained activity concerned with conceptual analysis, articulating transcendental conditions of possibility, developing truth conditions, or simply promoting and continuing an intellectual "conversation." These activities could even be carried out in an arcane language familiar only to other initiates. Dewey will have none of this turning away from the world of ordinary existence.

Intelligence in operation involves responsibility, not the escape from peril. Philosophy is that area of concern which welcomes the full brunt and burden of such accountability.

In order to emphasize this point, Dewey reinterprets the etymological definition of philosophy, "love of wisdom," apart from Modern connotations that associated wisdom with a detached, spectatorial rationality. The descriptive discipline of metaphysics provides the ground-map with which philosophy operates. But such a ground map is only a prerequisite to wisdom. "Love of wisdom is concerned with finding its implications for the conduct of life, in devotion to what is good" (LW 1:50).

For Plato, the highest idea, which, like the sun, suffused all of existence was the idea of the "Good." Dewey claimed that Platonic texts were his "favorite philosophic reading" (LW 5:154). In terms of the pervasive concern with good, Dewey was a follower of Plato as well. For empirical naturalism, concern for the good is the central and controlling end in view of the philosophical enterprise.

Humans, are "naturally philosophic, rather than metaphysical or coldly scientific, noting and describing" (LW 1:50). The noting and describing are not, however, opposed to the naturally philosophic temperament. Metaphysics, cognizance of the generic traits of existence, provides the "ground-map" in light of which the human project of enlarging goods can optimally take place. The sciences, by revealing the structures and relations of nature, provide the instrumentalities of control which give humans greater ability to utilize the forces of nature in the service of increased well-being. The challenge of philosophy "concerns the *interaction* of our judgments about ends to be sought with knowledge of the means for attaining them" (LW 4:30).

The aim of harmonizing "knowledge and practice" is the "securer, freer, more widely shared embodiment of values in experience by means of that active control of objects which knowledge alone makes possible" (LW 4:30). The fruit of philosophy is the wide dissemination of intrinsic goods. If companionship and communication are, as Dewey believed them to be, natural intrinsic goods, then one task of philosophy will be to insure that they are preserved to the degree in which they now exist, and are extended beyond the limitations within which they are presently constricted.

This activity which is central to philosophy has a name. Dewey calls it "criticism," understood in its etymological sense as appraisal or evaluation. Life-experience goes on regardless of whether we make the effort to guide it or not. It can, in other words, be either aphilosophical or properly philosophical.

> Some (experienced situations) take place with only a mini-mum of regulation, with little foresight, preparation and intent. Others occur because, in part, of the prior occur-rence of intelligent action. Both kinds are *had*; they are undergone, enjoyed or suffered. The first are not known; they are not understood; they are dispensations of fortune or providence. The second have, as they are experienced, meanings that present the funded outcome of operations that substitute definite continuity for experienced disconti-nuity and for the fragmentary quality due to isolation. (LW 4:194)

"Criticism" identifies that activity which seeks to minimize human dependence on the "dispensations of fortune or provi-dence." There is a certain givenness to existence, a "grain against which we cannot go" (MW 11:50). Yet existence is not rigidly fixed and inflexible. Our efforts can win for us modifications that will enhance existence. Democracy's allowance of increased free-dom to participate in the diverse activities of a society is one such enhancement. Any result of this sort will have begun with criticism. "Criticism is discriminating judgment, careful appraisal, and judgment is appropriately termed criticism when-ever the subject-matter of discrimination concerns goods and values" (LW 1:298).

The focus on "goods and values" is what makes criticism the culminating activity of philosophy. The affairs which make up life-experience include aspects which are inherently satisfying and fulfilling. Intelligently determined goods can become part of ordinary experience. But lived experience as contextual/tempo-ral is marked by change, precariousness, and unforseen conse-quences. Within such a context, criticism is the appropriate and natural response of that creature who, following the dictate of Socrates, ought to distinguish between living and living well.

> Possession and enjoyment of goods passes insensibly and inevitably into appraisal. First and immature experience is content simply to enjoy. But a brief course in experience enforces reflection; it requires but a brief time to teach that

some things sweet in the having are bitter in aftertaste and in what they lead to. Primitive innocence does not last. Enjoyment ceases to be a datum and becomes a problem. As a problem, it implies intelligent inquiry into the conditions and consequences of a value-object; that is, criticism. (LW 1:298)

The challenge of human life is to secure and extend those goods which are appropriate while discerning and overcoming the attraction of deceptive goods. This challenge can be addressed by criticism, "intelligent inquiry into the conditions and consequences of a value-object." Examination of consequences allows us to determine whether what is immediately experienced as good is genuinely valuable for human existence. The study of conditions helps us select modes of action that will optimize the presence of certain goods. The primary concern of philosophy within the framework of empirical naturalism is to "clarify, liberate and extend the goods which inhere in the naturally generated functions of experience" (LW 1:305). This activity is "criticism" which explains why Dewey characterizes philosophy as "inherently criticism, having its distinctive position among various modes of criticism in its generality; a criticism of criticisms as it were" (LW 1:298).

3

Democracy

Winthrop, Locke, and Dewey

The *Arbella* is not as famous a ship as is the *Mayflower*, which preceded it to the New World by a decade. Yet with regard to the ideals which were to guide the political life in the newly established colonies, the *Arbella's* stature is second to none. During its sailing across the Atlantic, John Winthrop, first governor of "The Company of Massachusetts Bay in New England," delivered a famous sermon. This sermon articulated Winthrop's vision of common life in the soon-to-be-established Puritan community. He stressed three interwoven themes: difference, cooperation, and justice. The dominant images he employed were those of a "fabric knit together" and "brotherhood." Notably absent from his discourse were two themes which have come to dominate the subsequent political life of the country, freedom and equality.

Indeed, Winthrop began by stressing inequality and diversity. The variety and difference among people was not an unfortunate fact to which humans must resign themselves. It was rather a sign of God's infinite greatness. Politically, such a manifestation was significant because it meant "that every man might have need of other, and from hence they might be all knitt more nearly together in the Bond of brotherly affeccion" (Winthrop, 23). Such an interlocking community required a special commitment of its members. Merely formal applications of judicial codes preserving public order would be insufficient. The inhabitants would need to take an active interest in securing communal well-being.

> For this end wee must be knitt together in this worke as one man, . . . wee must be willing to abridge ourselves of our superfluities, for the supply of others necessities, wee must uphold a familiar Commerce together in all meeknes, gentlenes, patience and liberality. (Winthrop, 26)

Winthrop's exhortations of personal sacrifice for the common weal indicated a special understanding of what is meant by community. It is not a mere agglomeration of individuals who happen to share geographic boundaries and a legal code. Winthrop's colony was to work together, "uphold a familiar Commerce together" so as to realize the substantive goal of communal well-being.

Equality and freedom, as we popularly understand them, were absent from Winthrop's vision because they would detract from his community's ideals. Equality understood as implying any sort of homogeneity would have meant an unwarranted tinkering with God's creation, a prideful substitution of human artifice for divine providence. Freedom, as escaping the constraints of living under a king sympathetic to Catholicism, was indeed a prerequisite for the new colony. But freedom defined primarily as absence of constraints would not have served the commonwealth. Transforming liberty into "liberality," generosity "for the supply of others necessities," was the new community's challenge. Answering such a challenge would be hindered, not helped, by a sense of liberty that would, too readily, become the province of the libertine.

Some sixty years later, John Locke promulgated a political vision that seems separated from Winthrop's by centuries rather than decades. *The Second Treatise of Government* focuses almost exclusively on freedom and equality. Notably absent from this text are the substantive ideals that were central to the sermon on the *Arbella*. Winthrop had spoken of a community knit together in brotherhood, each supplying the necessities of the other. Locke emphasized individual property and its preservation. Winthrop welcomed natural diversity and inequality. Locke asserted an original "*State of Perfect Equality*" (Locke, 290). Winthrop looked forward to the emerging community devoted to social well-being. Locke looked backward to the pristine freedom within the state of nature which justified in man the power to "preserve his Property" (Locke, 341).

The difference between the positions of these two men can be attributed, to a great degree, to their differing aims. Winthrop was faced with the task of providing a blueprint for the new colony. He sought to create a viable religiously centered community. His general source of inspiration was a decidedly pre-Modern text, the Bible. Locke's aim was different. He sought to undermine the justification for absolute monarchy, while providing a framework for majority rule and limited government. To these ends, Locke wove together a thoroughly Modern political doctrine which was built on the foundation of independent individuals in the state of nature.

Some two centuries after Locke, another John, the subject of this book, took up political questions. Like Winthrop and Locke, his reflections were occasioned by the historical context within which he found himself. Dewey lived through a period of rapid change. He was born during the Civil War, came of age during a period of massive immigration, saw America become an urban and industrial nation, lived through two world wars, and died at the beginning of the nuclear age. It is little wonder that an emphasis on change is a *leitmotif* permeating his entire work. In relation to Locke and Winthrop, the fruits of Dewey's reflections can be summarized as follows. The gap that separates Winthrop from Locke need not be as deep as it at first appears. Empirical naturalism offers a network of ideas within which the democratic aspirations of Locke can be coordinated with the concrete communal ideals of Winthrop. Dewey's rethinking of political theory moves beyond both pre-Modern and Modern political theory. It involves a fundamental retranslation of political terminology. "Democracy," "individual," "freedom," "equality," and "the public," take on new significance as they are woven into the new philosophical fabric.

This and the subsequent chapter will take up these themes, which are central to Dewey's reworking of political philosophy. His understanding of democracy, freedom, and equality will be covered in the present chapter. The next will deal with an issue that especially concerned Dewey: How to provide the conditions that encourage the establishment and self-awareness of a citizenry that participates fruitfully in directing the nation's course. This was an especially pressing challenge in a large, pluralistic, technologically advanced society. Responding to Walter Lippmann's charge that such a "public" was a "phantom," Dewey sought to present the conditions under which it could be revived.

Conjoint, Communicated Experience

The irony of Dewey's renown as America's most famous philosopher is that he espouses little of what has stereotypically become associated with the American character. Shane, Philip Marlowe, and Sam Spade fix the contours of the stereotype: an individual with no roots and little connectedness to community, someone for whom will is more important than reason, and ends justify the means; a highly competitive individual fixated on narrow purposes whose practice is marked by expedience rather than conventional morality. This picture of a competitive, rugged individual, someone committed to action rather than reflection represented the very type of "practical" ideal which Dewey's "pragmatism" sought to reform.[1] When democratic aspirations are woven into the fabric of empirical naturalism, a different more Winthrop-like type emerges as the exemplar of American democratic life.

Dewey's reformulation of democracy is analogous to his revisions in the philosophy of knowledge. In this respect he moves one step beyond another harsh critic of Modern epistemology, Karl Popper. Popper sought to separate Modern political theory, which he celebrated, from Modern epistemology, which he condemned. Modern epistemology may have been flawed, but it spawned "an intellectual and moral revolution without parallel in history" (Popper, 8). The political benefits that accompanied the flawed epistemology included the rejection of censorship, the introduction of individualism, a sense of human dignity, and the demand for universal education. All in all, according to Popper, "it is a case of a bad idea inspiring many good ones" (Popper, 8).

Dewey agrees that the inheritance from modernity was mixed. Unlike Popper, however, he suggests that *both* the epistemology and the political theory need to be revised. Indeed, both were skewed in analogous ways. It is important that these limitations be recognized lest the commendable aspirations of modernity remain frustrated in practice. "The democratic practice of life," Dewey wrote in 1919, "has been at an immense disadvantage. Prevailing philosophies have unconsciously discountenanced it" (MW 11:52). These prevailing philosophies have had as one of their results the creation of the Shane/Marlowe/Spade stereotype.

Recapturing the democratic ideal in its fullness requires locating its aspirations properly within the nexus of ideas that make up empirical naturalism. The "immense disadvantage" identified by Dewey resulted from the constraints placed upon "the democratic practice of life" by modernity's embrace of the Plotinian Temptation and the Galilean Purification. This embrace was manifested in its predilection for first positing isolated, ultimate simples, and then declaring them as foundational. We have already seen how Dewey called this procedure the "intellectualist" fallacy, one example of which is the empiricist fascination with "sense data."

Transferred to political philosophy, this attitude surfaces in the views of social contract theorists who posited the existence of isolated individuals in the state of nature. This bias misled political theorists like Locke into assuming as prototypical, an original, presocial situation inhabited by what might be called "precontextual, completed selves." They were imagined to be autonomous beings, possessing a fully developed faculty of reason. This reason made them clear-sighted about their interests. Their special situation meant that they enjoyed both freedom and equality.

Once the notion of antecedently existing completed selves, endowed with equality and freedom, is accepted, political discourse is channelled in a particular direction. Within such a context the act of formal entry into any sociopolitical association is viewed as a fundamental abandonment of the original freedom and equality. Political discourse then focuses on the question of how the original liberty can be protected in the new social arrangement. The topic of the individual *versus* the society then comes to be a primary concern. Within such a context, democratic aspirations gravitate toward securing more autonomy for the individual. The individual whose autonomy is maximal, living in a state whose powers are minimal, such are the two foci in the Modern version of democratic ideals.

Deweyan democratic theory, not allied to the assumptions of Modern empiricism, resituates political discourse outside of the milieu which occasions this formulation of sociopolitical alternatives. Empirical naturalism, as we saw in the last two chapters, neither succumbs to the Plotinian Temptation nor is it misled by the Galilean Purification. It regards ultimate simples as creations of an abstracting intelligence, not the givens of experience. The data of lived experience are not ultimate simples. The givens are rather the "situations," those complex, temporally conditioned events whose components are integrally related to one another.

Following the penchant for artificially isolated simples, theorists like Locke assumed that societies were composed of individuals. So commonsensical a claim might seem immune from criticism. Viewed from a Deweyan perspective, however, the claim can be challenged as misleadingly incomplete. Empirical naturalism, with its emphasis on the concrete, allows the recognition of a more thorough claim: societies are composed of individuals-in-interaction. An eighteenth-century mechanistic understanding of the world could easily lead thinkers to construe of society in "atomic" terms, that is, composed of indivisible, self-contained units. Dewey, influenced by biology, offers a conception of society that I would call "cellular." A society is made up of smaller societies. The ultimate constituents, like cells, are themselves composite and porous to the surrounding environment.

The social contract view was a fable constructed in light of dominant philosophical prejudices and with the specific and laudable end of limiting absolute power. The kinds of individuals described in the state of nature bear an uncanny resemblance to the eighteenth-century reformers themselves: educated, articulate, with clearly defined interests. The world in which Dewey lived, that of the late nineteenth and early twentieth centuries, presented altered conditions and novel problems. Reformers were no longer faced with the challenge of liberating the burgeoning mercantile class from suffocation by outmoded aristocratic rules and practices. The mercantile class had now become dominant, and a new challenge arose for reformers, liberating the impoverished laborer and the urban slum dweller.[2] Eighteenth-century theory appeared, in the newer light, as more and more inadequate and in need of revision.

For democratic aspirations to be embodied in practice, they have to be coordinated with a proper understanding of the human condition. Two important consequences result when democratic ideals are filtered through the twentieth-century orientation of empirical naturalism, rather than that of eighteenth century empiricism:

1. The realization of democratic ideals cannot be premised on the supposed preexistence of individuals as completed selves in a state of nature.
2. Democratic principles must be brought to life within a human context which is inherently and ineluctably social.

What results is an understanding of democratic life that may not quite match Winthrop's exhortation to "abridge ourselves of our superfluities for the supply of others necessities." It does, however, involve paying attention to the multiple implications of our actions on those with whom we share community life. Democracy, says Dewey, is "more than a form of government." It is, fundamentally, a "mode of associated living, of conjoint communicated experience." This emphasis on the social dimension of democracy means that a special responsibility befalls democratic citizens: thinking through the implications of our actions for others before engaging in them.

> The extension in space of the number of individuals who participate in an interest so that each had to refer his own action to that of others, and to consider the action of others to give point and direction to his own, is equivalent to the breaking down of those barriers of class, race, and national territory which kept men from perceiving the full import of their activity. (MW 9:93)

Democracy, for Dewey, represents the ideal manifestation of community life. Establishing a democratic community requires the awareness that sociality, living in association with others, is not simply a restrictive condition. It is both limiting and enhancing. Being part of a community provides opportunities for growth as well as the conditions for constraint. The answer to oppression is not an escape from association, but the effort, a concrete, empirically grounded effort, to reform the types of association so as to produce the optimal conditions for growth within them. Toward such an end, there are no fixed, atemporal, absolute formulae. It may be necessary at a certain time characterized by certain social conditions and problems, to limit state power. Under others, it may be necessary to expand it.

As Dewey pointed out in a passage cited above, democracy is "more than a form of government." It is not to be identified with particular constitutions or legal systems. Actually existing practices, whether carrying the label "democratic" or not, must always be distinguished from the democratic ideal. The former are means. As such they are flexible and must be constantly evaluated in light of the latter. What are the criteria by which alleged democratic practices may be judged? Dewey provided a clear statement in *The Public and its Problems*.

> From the standpoint of the individual, it consists in having a responsible share according to capacity in forming and directing the activities of the groups to which one belongs

and in participating according to need in the values which
the groups sustain. From the standpoint of the groups, it
demands liberation of the potentialities of members of a
group in harmony with the interests and goods which are
common. Since every individual is a member of many
groups, this specification cannot be fulfilled except when
different groups interact flexibly and fully in connection
with other groups. (LW 2: 327–28)

The immediate background against which democratic aspirations emerged was the aristocratic society of fixed classes,
guided by a king whose will was law. The first principle of democracy, as etymology suggests, is providing means for giving power
to the people, not to an individual or to a restricted class. But the
people in question are always people-in-associations, people
already part of various groupings.

This realization, stressed by Dewey in the last citation, suggests specific criteria for determining the degree to which a society is moving in the direction of the democratic ideal.

1. It must allow "a responsible share according to capacity" in
    the direction of policy.
2. The society needs to be so managed that it and the groups
    that make it up, encourage and actively elicit the develop-
    ment of powers latent in their members. Democracy
    "demands liberation of the potentialities of members of a
    group."
3. Finally, a society moves in the direction of the democratic
    ideal when the varied groups that compose it have relations
    that are multiple and supple, "when different groups interact
    flexibly and fully." The more porous are the boundaries of
    such groups, the more, in other words, they welcome par-
    ticipation from all individuals, and the more the varied
    groupings enjoy multiple and flexible relations, the closer
    is a society to fulfilling the democratic ideal.

On the Deweyan scheme, complacency about presently
existing structures becomes difficult, if not impossible. We are
never able to identify a particular constitution and a particular
set of practices with the once-and-for-all manifestation of democracy. Whatever are the present conditions, they must be examined from the triple perspective of whether (1) participation in for-

mulating policy is widespread, (2) latent talents find the conditions for their development, and (3) relations between social groups are fluid. In its perfect sense, democracy "is not a fact and never will be." Nonetheless, without a guiding ideal we would never engage in the work to eliminate the "restrictive and disturbing elements" which prevent a fuller flowering of democratic life (LW 2:328).

A Deweyan evaluative schema removes democratic discourse from the orbit it has had for the last two centuries. So prominent was this orbit, that political foes such as Marxists and libertarians can both be found to have their trajectories affected by it. Karl Marx's "withering away of the state" and the libertarian ideal of a "minimal state" both depend on the imagined ideal of original autonomous individuals in the state of nature. In the same vein, the exhortation of sixties' students to "do your own thing," represents merely another satellite orbiting the same center.

Once the philosophical center is changed, the ideal of "do your own thing" can be recognized as an articulation of precisely what democracy is not. Democracy is "primarily a mode of associated living." It is a way of living together characterized by "conjoint communicated experience." This means that the primary responsibility of democratic citizens is concern with the development of shared interests that lead to sensitivity about repercussions of actions on others. "Do your own thing" was a sixties incarnation of the nineteenth-century industrialist's demand for maximal individual autonomy.

In its most vibrant sense, democracy provides an ideal of community life in which citizens engage in social discourse to determine how projected actions will impact on others. Too often the democratic state is understood as simply providing a set of rules which allow individuals the widest latitude within which they may do as they wish. For Dewey, this is not the primary function of democratic community life. A vibrant community will seek to create a context of criss-crossing and zig-zagging interests that are made public and communally discussed so that policy will result, not from individual acts of will, but from "conjoint communicated experience."

Dewey believes that the realization of democratic life is a challenge requiring constant effort and attention. It cannot be reduced to the slogan "Leave me alone." Instead of thinking in terms of our own aims in isolation, it urges that these be scrutinized for their impact on our co-citizens. The demand of democratic life is to encourage the creation of social interests such that "each had to refer his own action to that of others," and that "different groups interact flexibly and fully in connection with other groups."

We are not, save in special cases, isolated individuals. Our actions respond to those of others, as well as extend from us in concentric circles affecting others. Democracy as an ideal for community life is not a mere provision for a minimal state which simply leaves citizens alone. Such an individualistic ideal is inimical to the kind of associated living which is democratic. This kind of community life ought to occasion a sensitivity to the consequences of one's actions. It should, in other words, extend participation and awareness. "The clear consciousness of a communal life, in all its implications, constitutes the idea of democracy" (LW 2:328).

Freedom as Growth

The social contract fable occasioned an understanding of humans as already complete, mature selves in full possession of faculties for rational judgment. Empirical naturalism, by contrast, understands the self as a continually emerging product. It is not antecedently given and fixed. Temporality and relations enter into the very constitution of the individual. What we are, what we become, is due, in large measure, to the particular trajectory which our life takes.

If this understanding of human nature is correct, then, once again, democratic practice must involve more than merely separating the individual from constraining conditions. Such an isolationist ideal makes good sense when completed selves are assumed as perfectly representative of the citizenry. If we were all the antecedently completed selves suggested by Locke, the ideal of freedom as autonomy might be feasible and comprehensive. The fact is that this fable misrepresents the human condition. There is no completed self requiring only elimination of extraneous conditions to reveal itself. Humans are open-ended creatures, shaped and influenced by the cultures they inhabit, the languages they speak, and the relations into which they enter.

For this reason, "growth" becomes a controlling ideal by which democratic societies can be judged.

> Democracy has many meanings, but if it has a moral mean-
> ing, it is found in resolving that the supreme test of all polit-
> ical institutions and industrial arrangements shall be the
> contribution they make to the all-around growth of every
> member of society. (MW 12:186)

"Growth" is not to be confused with *self*-development conceived as
the movement to a preordained goal. Growth means rather the
continual flowering and actualizing of possibilities. As such it is a
substantive, concrete process. Growth involves the actual
enhancement of an individual's life. It signifies the development of
new powers of action. The kind of liberation called forth by democracy cannot then be simply the procedural one of being left alone
from the interference of others. Freedom involves something more
concrete: the emergence of effective powers of action. Until the
actual realization of capacities, not just the preconditions for such
realization, exists, democratic life will be partial and unfulfilled.

A precondition for such fulfillment involves rejecting the political version of the Galilean Purification: the eighteenth century's
"individual in isolation." Empirical naturalism's more inclusive
description would identify "individuals-in-interaction." Such a concrete avowal of complex relatedness means that both the social
dimension of life and its temporality are better appreciated.

James had followed this path as it applied to the question of
truth. In so doing, he had stressed the literal meaning of veri-
fication, the process of "making" truth (James, 1981, 92). Truths,
in other words, do not preexist as fully articulated. They may
refer to natural operations, but their articulations do not pre-
exist, waiting simply for the human spectator to espy them. It
takes inquiry, effort, reflection, and tentative formulations before
natural operations can be translated into humanly structured
hypotheses. In turn, the truth or falsity of such hypotheses can
only be ascertained by processes of veri-fication.

Similarly we can say that for Dewey, two major challenges of
democracy involve *liberti-fication* and *egali-fication*. Neither freedom nor equality is an antecedently given, fully formed characteristic of human life. Both require appropriate conditions and
concerted effort for their emergence.

To understand Dewey properly with regard to freedom, this
emphasis on "making" must be kept in mind. Freedom "is something to be achieved," it is not "an original possession" (LW 2:61).
Social contract theorists like Locke and Rousseau differed on

many issues, but they were one in assuming that the individual, prior to association in states, was free. This was the primitive data with which they began.

Modern epistemology, as Popper properly remarked, believed that truth would be "manifest" if only the distorting factors of traditional philosophies, cultural prejudices, and distrustful perceptions could be overcome. In an analogous manner, Modern political theorists held that freedom, a primordial possession of humanity, would also manifest itself fully were it not for the inconvenience of having to live with others in politically ordered communities.

When Dewey asserted that the moral meaning of democracy was associated with "growth" he signalled an important departure from eighteenth-century assumptions. "Growth" is a carefully selected term. Readers must resist the temptation to treat it as synonymous with either *self*-development or *self*-realization. The latter expressions are too intimately linked with the ontology of monadic individualism. *Self*-development readily connotes either a preordained process toward an antecedently determined end, or the sort of trajectory which can be undertaken in isolation. By contrast, Dewey intends growth to signify (1) genuine contingency, and (2) contextuality.[3]

Self-realization might be construed as occurring apart from or even in spite of interactions. Growth cannot be so construed. It is a process that issues out of varied associations. The kind of growth, its direction and quality, all depend on the sort of associated activities within which we participate.

Too often, freedom is simply understood as absence of constraints. Remove the restrictions, a Locke or a Mill tell us, and humans will be free. This is true, replies Dewey, only for well-educated, articulate individuals like Locke and Mill. Their error was to generalize too readily from what was a privileged perspective.

> They (classical liberals) thought of individuals as endowed with an equipment of fixed and ready-made capacities, the operation of which if unobstructed by external restrictions would be freedom which would almost automatically solve political and economic problems. (LW 3:99)

In other words, the classical liberals committed the fallacy of intellectualism. They read back as part of some supposed original condition what were actually the results of upbringing, education, and experience. Removing political and social restrictions would surely increase *their* powers for executing plans of action. This did not mean, however, that (1) such powers could be treated as a natural endowment, and (2) removing restrictions was a sufficient precondition for the flowering of freedom in all citizens.[4]

Because he was sensitive to such limitations, Dewey does not, when he speaks of freedom, mean it in the sense which the term has come to have in ordinary discourse, mere absence of restraints. This meaning, which has become usual since the eighteenth century, is a misleading oversimplification. It represents but one condition for what Dewey calls "effective" freedom. "Effective" freedom is the actual ability to carry out a course of action. It signifies the "power to frame purposes, to judge wisely, to evaluate desires by the consequences which will result from acting upon them; power to select and order means to carry chosen ends into operation" (LW 13:41).

Freedom in this sense cannot be identified with simply removing restrictions, what Dewey refers to as "purely formal" liberty (LW 11:27). The gap between democratic ideals and their realization is partially occasioned by an impoverished conception of freedom. "Because the liberals failed to make a distinction between purely formal or legal liberty and effective liberty of thought and action, the history of the last one hundred years is the history of the non-fulfillment of their predictions" (LW 11: 27).

Freedom is not an all-or-nothing power, existing either full-blown or not at all. Such an understanding ignores the temporal, developmental character of human life. Effective freedom can be increased, or it can be minimized, depending on social conditions. The mere absence of restrictions is not sufficient for growth in effective freedom. Discipline, training, effort, and opportunity are also required. Without the latter, freedom remains "purely formal," an empty possibility, not the realized capability for carrying out a course of action.

Were I to say, for example, "I am free to speak Spanish," this might, in the ordinary, purely formal understanding of the phrase, mean simply "I live in a society where neither laws nor social proscriptions forbid me from speaking the language." On this meaning, everyone living in such a society could make the same claim. Each of its citizens could say "I am free to speak Spanish," even those unable to converse in the language. This is the sense in which freedom is "purely formal." "I am free" means only that no external, official restraint on such a behavior exists. It does not signify the positive capacity to carry out the desired course of action.

Effective freedom, by contrast, does mean the concrete capacity to carry out a course of action. The claim "I am free to speak Spanish," in its fullest sense, means that, given the opportunity, I could actually carry on a conversation. In the concrete world of practice, not the abstract world of formal possibility, I am *not* free merely because socio-legal restraints are absent. I am free when I can converse intelligibly with someone.

Classical liberals were wrong to conceive of freedom as something that exists antecedently and can be made manifest by the simple removal of restrictions. It is a capacity that may be developed through time and in conjunction with the aid of others. Freedom as growth in powers of effective action cannot emerge in a context that is merely free from interference. Indeed, increasing "effective" freedom often requires others (as mentors, teachers, suppliers of materials) and constraint (in the form of discipline, effort, and practice).

Traditional eighteenth- and nineteenth-century liberals failed to sort out what was merely one condition of freedom with the fuller sense of what freedom in practice would really mean. They too readily generalized on the basis of their own unique situations. The bourgeoisie, literate and able in commerce, required only the removal of artificial restrictions for it to take an active place in the social hierarchy. Their situation was akin to those who, already speaking Spanish, live in a society where the use of the language is forbidden. Eliminating the restriction is all they require for putting the activity into practice. But the mere lifting of the ban would not make those previously incapable of speaking the language automatically fluent. To say that these latter are as "free" as the former is to abuse the concrete, full meaning of the term.

Thinking within the context of the bourgeoisie held back by antiquated restrictions, eighteenth-century political theorists focused on what was immediately important to them, removal of those obstacles. The result was that the mere removal of constraints "did have a liberating effect upon such individuals as were antecedently possessed of the means, intellectual and economic, to take advantage of the changed social conditions." The main political consequence of their efforts was the emancipation of "the *classes* whose special interests they represented rather than human beings impartially" (LW 3:100).

What they unconsciously assumed was that the elimination of restrictions could be universalized as a satisfactory understanding of freedom. They failed to recognize that for many of their co-citizens, effective freedom could not be achieved without the establishment of appropriate social instrumentalities, among the most prominent of which was free public education. "No man and no mind," Dewey argued, "was ever emancipated merely by being left alone" (LW 2:340).

Empirical naturalism so alters the paradigm for discussing freedom that a well-regarded ideal rooted in the eighteenth century, "autonomy," has to be reexamined. So long as autonomy is viewed as representing the goal associated with freedom, the full impact of the Deweyan critique will not be felt.

The philosophers of modernity tended to fear connection and dependence. Even today, these words maintain slightly negative connotations. Both connection and dependence are thought of merely in their restrictive dimensions. Empirical naturalism allows a rehabilitation of these terms as prerequisites for effective freedom. Interconnection and interdependence are irrecusable facts of human experience. Their limiting dimensions are balanced off by the opportunities for genuine growth which they also provide. A philosophy which ignores this, or substitutes for it an artificial anthropology, will distort the ideal of human freedom, thereby hampering, rather than enhancing the actual development of freedom in individuals.

Empirical naturalism, by assuming the primacy of interactions, moves beyond eighteenth century assumptions. "Association in the sense of connection and combination is a 'law' of everything known to exist. Singular things act, but they act together" (LW 2:250). If the Deweyan grasp of things is correct, we must, in order to foster growth, pursue associations, not shun them. Humans should not seek autonomy, but rather freedom as the increased powers of effective action. Such freedom can only emerge from the proper sorts of associations with and dependencies on others.

Using the terms "connection" and "dependence" in a nonpejorative sense sounds strange to our ears because we still live in the shadow of modernity. Only if we embrace the assumptions of eighteenth-century philosophy will connection and dependence be considered solely as constraints or limits. These faulty assumptions led to the coining of a new term "autonomy" to indicate a human ideal. But such a perspective on freedom was, according to Dewey, a misconstrual of the liberation so eagerly sought. This liberation was not the "absurdity of striving to be free from connection with nature and one another." The eighteenth-century fascination with feral children should have been instructive. Disconnection meant retrogression, not progress in effective powers of action. The aspiration was rather "for greater freedom *in* nature and society." What was sought was "not isolation from the world, but a more intimate connection with it" (MW 9:302–3).

Fuller freedom cannot be secured if it is considered to be inconsistent with dependence, connection, and association. Quite the contrary is the case. Freedom as genuine power to carry out selected activities can only be developed in and through association with others. "To view institutions as enemies of freedom, and all conventions as slaveries, is to deny the only means by which positive freedom in action can be secured" (MW 14:115).

We owe a great deal to the eighteenth- and nineteenth-century philosophers who bequeathed to us the Modern ideal of democracy. Our gratitude should not blind us, however, to the limitations that attach to their views. The state of nature imagery within which they worked, their commitment to an ontology of ultimate simples, their assumption that what they required for the exercise of freedom was identical to what everyone would require, and their assumption of freedom as a full-blown, ready-made property, led to their one-sided understanding of freedom as autonomy.

Autonomy as a model for freedom leads in practice to separation from others, not toward democratic community. Deweyan concrete freedom encourages individuals to seek out the proper sorts of association. These are not thought of one-dimensionally as simply imposing restrictions. Indeed, the exact opposite is the case. They are sought in the name of securing greater powers of effective action, that is, greater freedom. "A *distinctive* way of behaving in conjunction and *connection* with other distinctive ways of acting, not a self-enclosed way of acting, independent of everything else, is that toward which we are pointed" (LW 2:353).

Marriage, school, trade associations, social organizations, political groups, athletic leagues and labor unions all provide opportunities for *increasing* one's freedom. They allow us to move concretely toward accomplishments which would not be possible outside of such relations. Only when we think of freedom as a full-blown antecedent property does it make sense to complain that social connections are uniquely constraining and to idealize "autonomous" individuals. When democratic liberty is understood in its connection with growth in powers of effective action, humans will no longer feel the need to contrast themselves as isolated individuals with themselves as members of associations. They will rather judge and modify the various sorts of affiliations in light of whether these favor or obstruct increased freedom.[5]

Equality as Individuality

Not surprisingly, empirical naturalism will challenge prevailing views of equality in a manner similar to its understanding of freedom. John Locke could set down authoritatively the claim that the original state of human nature was a *"State of perfect Freedom . . . A State* also *of Equality"* (Locke, 287). This seminal democratic theorist treats both freedom and equality as original and complete possessions. As we have seen with the question of freedom, Dewey's empirical naturalism, accepting as it does the temporal, interactive milieu of human life, denies this assumption. With regard to freedom, Dewey stressed the process of "growth." His interpretation of democratic equality emphasizes "individuality."

The case of equality poses special challenges to the philosopher. There exists a ready-made and prominent interpretive framework, the quantitative, within which one understanding of equality offers itself for generalization. Such a quantitative reading of equality would indicate that whatever the particular subject of discussion (e.g. talent, wealth, physical powers), equality would mean a similar distribution among all members of the society. This reading of equality is so counterintuitive, however, that it cannot be seriously entertained. As Winthrop well recognized, variety, diversity, and inequality are inevitable accompaniments of any human society.

Locke himself had provided the first suggestion for modifying the quantitative, all-or-nothing understanding of equality. He readily admitted that there were many respects—for example, age, merit, virtue, duty—which mitigated the claim that "all men by nature are equal" (Locke, 322). He also recognized the developmental nature of equality by admitting that children "are not born in this full state of *Equality*, though they are born to it" (Locke, 322). Nonetheless, such qualifications remain the exception in the *Second Treatise*, which reverts time and again to the claim that equality is an original possession.

As in the case of freedom, Dewey denies that equality is an original possession. Equality, however, provides Dewey with a more daunting challenge than did freedom. Freedom as growth, liberti-fication as an ongoing goal of democratic societies, makes sense when the positive, incremental sense of freedom is explained. Egali-fication is another matter. Must not equality be in some sense a precondition for democratic life? Must not any attempt at egali-fication lead inexorably to the homogenization of society?

These difficulties are met head on by Dewey because there is a sense in which his political philosophy is an attempt to graft Locke onto Winthrop. He is as convinced as was Winthrop, that difference is unavoidable and irreducible. At the same time, he is certain, like Locke, that equality is an important democratic ideal.

How is Dewey's hybrid to be construed? "Individuality" is that onto which he fastens to breed this hybrid. The role played by growth-into-enablement in the understanding of freedom will now be played by growth-into-individuality with regard to equality. To understand what Dewey means by individuality and its role in reconceptualizing equality, it has first to be distinguished from its cognate, "individualism."

Individualism forms an integral component of empiricism's intellectual fabric, especially that thread which accepts ultimate simples as foundational. Within such a context, individuals can be imagined as self-sufficient subjects in the state of nature. They are assumed to exist as fully self-conscious beings, capable of reasonable decisions in light of their own interests. Two beliefs are thus central to individualism: (1) Humans are considered to be completed selves outside of association with others. (2) They are thought to be guided, if not solely, then most prominently, by self-interest.

Empirical naturalism, quite simply, replaces the threads with which such a view is woven. It attempts to preserve the best of the earlier position, while mitigating its overemphasis on selves in isolation from others. "Individuality" best suits the new fabric because it accentuates the social dimension in human life, while maintaining a suggestion of process and growth. At the same

FIGURE 3.1

John Dewey, New York, 1943

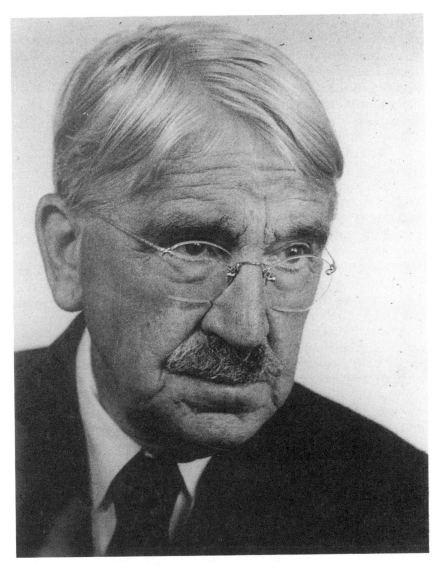

Courtesy of John Dewey Papers, Special Collections/Morris Library, Southern Illinois University at Carbondale.

time, it minimizes the emphasis on prior possession. "Only in the physical sense of physical bodies that to the senses are separate is individuality an original datum. Individuality in a social and moral sense is something to be wrought out" (MW 12:191).

What is it that is to be "wrought out?" Persons whose character, actions, and contributions cannot be reduced to those of anyone else. "Individuality" identifies the distinctive manner in which someone participates in communal life. It signifies uniqueness, irreplaceability. "Individualism" connotes both isolation and self-interestedness. It assumes the opposition of self and community. "Individuality," by contrast, suggests a mode of participation. It recognizes the irreducibility of community and the multiple interests associated with it.

What does all this have to do with equality? Equality is a manner of regarding others which refuses any absolute scale by which to judge them. People are equal in the sense that life offers multiple contexts within which to evaluate others. Democratic equality is postulated on the denial of any single, atemporal, universal context for judgment. It is thus linked to "incommensurability." "Moral equality means incommensurability, the inapplicability of common and quantitative standards" (MW 13:299).

On the quantitative model, "equality" would be a property of two elements that matched each other or matched an absolute standard. The yardsticks we use either are or are not equal in length to the standard kept in the bureau of weights and measures. Equality in this sense requires "co-mensurability," the capacity to measure a given instrument against the established, official, absolute standard.

In the democratic community, no such universal, pre-existing standards exist. To say that humans are equal is precisely to recognize the absence of such standards. "Equality" as incommensurability encourages the appreciation of diverse skills, talents, and contributions. It is for Dewey a way of recognizing the uniqueness of other human beings:

Equality does not signify that kind of mathematical or physical equivalence in virtue of which any one element may be substituted for another. It denotes effective regard for whatever is distinctive and unique in each, irrespective of physical and psychological inequalities. It is not a natural possession but is a fruit of the community when its action is directed by its character as a community. (MW 12:329–30)

Several important Deweyan themes converge in this passage.

1. There is the straightforward claim that equality is a result, a "fruit," not an antecedent possession. Without growth in individuality, without developing unique ways of contributing to communal projects, there is no political equality. There is only initial inequality, undisturbed and unmitigated.
2. The passage also highlights the important Deweyan theme of participation. Equality is a communal product. Like freedom, it cannot thrive when individuals are left alone. One's possibilities for making a contribution can only be cultivated if the appropriate social interactions take place.
3. Finally, there is the identification of equality with "whatever is distinctive and unique." Equality is not identity. To say, for example, that men and women are equal is not the same as to say that they are identical. The quantitative model of exact congruence, what Dewey elsewhere calls "mechanical identity" (LW 2:329), is wholly inappropriate to the political context. Democratic life fosters equality when opportunities are made real by "establishing the basic conditions through which and because of which every human being might become all that he was capable of becoming" (LW 11:168).

Given the Deweyan articulation of equality, it may seem that his understanding, although philosophically interesting, is idiosyncratic in that it has little in common with the ordinary connotations of the term. To close the gap between his formulation and ordinary usage, we need to recognize that the most prominent link is a negative one. Acceptance of equality means that blanket claims of superiority and inferiority are disallowed. Superiority and inferiority must always be related to a context: superior or inferior in which respects and to what ends?[6] The cultivation of individuality, which involves the kind of growth understood as freedom, calls forth a level of respect for each person. Political equality exists when there is no sociopolitical bureau of weights and measures providing a single scale against which all individuals are to be compared.

This is the point Dewey stresses by allying equality to incommensurability. The Plotinian Temptation toward a single standard is not absent from the political sphere. The world of commerce has, since the nineteenth century, provided the overriding context within which the standard for judging others is located. As Dewey points out, if it is assumed that all citizens are equally fitted for a single aim, the "power for attaining ends common to a class of competitors," the not surprising outcome will involve "putting a premium on mastery over others" (MW 13:299). Whether the single measure be thought of as attaining power and wealth in the world of commerce, or ranking high on a Kohlberg-type scale of moral development, the Plotinian Temptation to identify *one* scale has been embraced and assumed as controlling. Democratic equality, by contrast, is operative where it is admitted that there exists no single scale of values providing *the* evaluative scale for everyone. There is a plurality of standards and scales.

Such a view does not necessitate an overreaction in the direction of many contemporary thinkers who reject all hierarchies. Nor need empirical naturalism dismiss the importance of value judgments. There is no inherent contradiction between democratic equality and either hierarchies or value judgments. Inconsistency only arises when a single scale of values, a single hierarchy, is selected as providing *the* scale according to which humans are to be judged. Democratic equality, by contrast, requires that we seek out, identify, and appreciate the distinctive contributions of each person. Understood in this way, democracy preserves what was best in aristocracy. Dewey goes so far as to say that a properly understood democracy is "aristocracy carried to its limit." "It is a claim that every human being as an individual may be the best for some particular purpose and hence be the most fitted to rule, to lead, in that specific respect." There is one enemy of both genuine aristocracy and genuine democracy, the "habit of fixed and numerically limited classifications" (MW 13:297–98).

For Dewey, equality does not involve the assumption that somehow behind the appearances of difference, everyone is alike.[7] Nor does it signify that somehow we are all competitors lined up at the beginning of a single race. Democratic equality, rather, implies both the recognition and the encouragement of uniqueness. Equality as an ideal is precisely what prevents us from seeing all humans as alike. It means that no single end, activity, or approach can be judged as superior in a universal way. Equality as an ideal celebrates plurality and diversity. It means, according to Dewey "a world in which an existence must be reckoned with on its own account, not as something capable of equation with and transformation into something else" (MW 11:53).

To consider equality in any other manner would lead progressively toward the establishment of narrow and fixed categories of what counts as success. The practical result of this narrowing would be great inequities, since humans are not all disposed to compete for the same ends. In turn, this would give rise to the revival of what is always the danger to be avoided, a society polarized by fixed classes.

Humans do not begin as neutral blank slates on which a single model text is to be inscribed. They start out with varying possibilities and interests. The mechanic, the good parent, the carpenter, the laborer should not be looked down upon because they cannot meet the narrow criteria of a society focused on wealth as the measure of success. Democratic equality must avoid taking the position that everyone exists originally in a state of "mechanical identity." Rather, in line with empirical naturalism, "equality" becomes the impetus for refusing to impose narrow and rigid hierarchies upon emerging and emergent lives.

Unfairness, not fairness results when equality is treated as an original given. It then becomes too simple a matter for whatever group is dominant to proclaim that its ideals, standards, and aims should be those for everyone. Since everyone is assumed to have started out equally, those who have not succeeded are considered to be not only inferior, but inferior through some fault of their own. Self-esteem and self-image are bound to be battered in a society whose media celebrate a few models of success while ignoring or denigrating the rest. What results is too often a severe inequality which is especially perverse because it often passes itself off as based on the ideal of equality.

For Dewey, democratic life is difficult and challenging. It is not an easy path. Democracy requires vigilance, effort, and experimentation. The experimental spirit is important in order that democracies may always modify the means enacted toward the realization of the ideal. The danger of understanding freedom and equality in a non-Deweyan way is that of self-satisfaction or stagnation. The Deweyan emphasis, what I have called libertification and egali-fication, stresses rather the effort and struggle needed to realize democratic ideals.

Democracy is to be judged, not by a particular system of laws and institutions which arose in historical tandem with democratic theory. These are flexible means. A democracy should be judged by the way all of its citizens are able to develop their capacities and thus grow in effective freedom. It should be judged by the way it encourages individuality, the unique distinctive contributions its citizens are actually capable of making. Equality will then be a concrete present reality not the hollow echo from a mythical state of nature.

4

The Public

Mass or Public?

Writing in the late 1920s Jose Ortega y Gasset claimed that "Europe is suffering from the greatest crisis that can afflict peoples, nations, and civilization" (Ortega y Gasset, 11). What was this crisis? The ascension to power of "the masses." Why was it a crisis? The masses "neither should nor can direct their own personal existence, and still less rule society in general" (Ortega y Gasset, 11). How to face this crisis by preserving the gains of liberal democracy while minimizing its dangers was the task Ortega set for himself in *The Revolt of the Masses.*[1]

Had he been writing in the late eighteenth century, Ortega's focus might have been different. He might well have discussed a "revolt of the public." At that time, the threat to liberty would have come mainly from a corrupted monarchy and aristocracy. The champions of freedom would have celebrated the "public," a word derived from the Latin *populus*, people. The public, a widened version of what the Greeks called the *demos*, was, after all, the group deserving of power in the emerging democracies.

By the twentieth century, however, in an ironic inversion, Ortega suggested that the threat to democracy came from the "people" identified now, not as a "public," but as a "mass." A "mass," as its etymology indicates, is a lump or a heap of paste, something which, while not distinguished in itself, can easily be manipulated. The people as the "masses" are considered to be unthinking, prejudiced, intolerant. The great fear of Ortega, borne out within a generation, was that the masses would be easy prey for demagogues and thus basic ingredients for the emergence of totalitarianism.

The switch from "public" to "mass" as a way of identifying the *demos* is significant with respect to the development of democratic theory. In its most radical form the theory assumes that all citizens are equally competent to have a say and take part in public life. Pushed to its logical limits, democracy would pick its officials by lot, rotate them frequently, and even elect its military leaders, three procedures described by Aristotle in *The Athenian Constitution* (Aristotle, 2368–69).

The establishment of democratic "republics" signalled the recognition of the need to mitigate radical democratic theory in light of an effective, viable political organization. In this country, Madison had argued that a "pure" democracy "can admit of no cure for the mischief of factions," and that such democracies "have ever been the spectacles of turbulence and contention." "A republic," he claimed, "opens a different prospect, and promises the cure for which we are seeking." Such a republic would differ from a "pure" democracy in two ways: (1) those charged with running the government would form but a small portion of the entire citizenry; (2) a republic could spread itself over a greater area and include more citizens than a pure democracy (Madison, 224).

The United States into which Dewey was born had become larger geographically and more diverse ethnically than Madison could have imagined. No doubt, this would have reinforced, for Madison, the wisdom of establishing a republic instead of a pure democracy. Democratic realists have ever since tended to follow Madison in this regard. As societies become more complex, principles of organization are needed for effective governance. The inevitability of a specialized class which actually determines policy has come to be known as the "iron law of oligarchy."

This law derives from the early-twentieth-century German sociologist, Robert Michels, who felt reluctantly compelled, as a result of his research, to demolish "some of the facile and superficial democratic illusions which trouble science and lead the masses astray" (Michels, 368). Among the hard facts to be faced was the "objective immaturity of the mass" which resulted in the need for the "division of labor, specialization, and guidance" (Michels, 367). This led, in turn, to the creation of new oligarchies, "parties, that is to say, which are increasingly based upon the competence of the few" (Michels, 370).

Realists, accepting the inevitability of elites to run complex organizations, seek to modify democratic theory in order to accommodate this necessity. Pure democracy, as Madison had argued, is dangerous. In the complex contemporary world, Michels added, it is not even an option.

Because democratic theorists must always confront the same practical concerns as did Madison about the failures of prior attempts at establishing effective democracies, and because contemporary societies are so complex as to necessitate multiple levels of organization, realists seek for ways to integrate the necessity of elites into democratic theory. A popular textbook in political science speaks bluntly of the need for "elites" and the antidemocratic danger that is posed by the aroused "masses."

> Democratic theory assumes that liberal values—individual dignity, equality of opportunity, the right of dissent, freedom of speech and press, religious toleration, and due process of law—are best protected by the expansion and growth of mass political participation. Historically, the masses and not elites were considered the guardians of liberty. . . . But in the twentieth century, it has been the masses who have been most susceptible to the appeals of totalitarianism. (Dye and Zeigler, 14)

The problem, according to the authors, is that although "abstract expressions of democratic values" are supported, the masses are not "willing to translate abstract principles into democratic patterns of behavior" (Dye and Zeigler, 147). The masses are thought to be narrow-minded, willing to impose conformity of thought and behavior at the expense of personal liberties, and prone to violence.

The gap between "public" and "mass" provides a perspective from which to understand Dewey's reformulation of democratic theory. He is as sensitive as any democratic realist to the foibles and weaknesses of human nature. He does not believe that prejudice, dogmatism, authoritarianism, and hatred disappear by virtue of citizenship in a democratic nation. Nonetheless, he is most concerned that the ideal of a participatory citizenry not be dismissed too glibly.[2] One great challenge of the democratic experiment is that of cultivating a "public" thereby minimizing the dangers associated with a "mass."

The immediate context for Dewey's reflections was a book by Walter Lippmann, *The Phantom Public*, published in 1925. There, as in his earlier *Public Opinion* (1922), Lippmann argued that, for all intents and purposes, the traditional "public" was a phantom. Twentieth-century democratic societies should not continue to believe that eighteenth-century conditions still prevail. The picture of "omnicompetent" citizens deliberating on all of the major issues of the day, and then setting policy, was regularly gainsaid by actual practice.

The resolution of this contrast between theory and practice did not lie in simply readjusting practice to fit theory. Theory itself had to be reformulated. The complexity of life in the twentieth century would not allow an effective and successful society to flourish without decision-making by a set of elites. These would be individuals whose competence, training and impartiality made them best capable of understanding the intricacies of the complex problems facing them.

Because of greatly altered social and technological conditions, the older image of a democratic public had become obsolete. A country like the United States, characterized by its size, its advanced technology, and its pluralism, could no longer assume the appropriateness of traditional models for guidance. The Greek *polis*, Winthrop's commonwealth, and Jefferson's agrarian republic, were unsuitable as prototypes to be copied exactly in a pluralistic, industrialized, urbanized society.

On these older models, the public was tightly limited and readily identified. The public encompassed a group of citizens with shared social standing, homogeneity of tradition, and common objectives. These traits, in turn, encouraged citizen participation in formulating public policy. Under the altered contemporary conditions the public is a heterogeneous collection of individuals with little time for the depth of study needed to evaluate and act on the complex issues of the day. Because of this, the formulation of public policy could no longer emerge directly from the public.

Altered circumstances require the mediation of experts whose competence would be combined with a neutrality regarding the outcome of the policy (Lippmann, 1965, 250–57). The role of the public would be to depend on these experts. The public does not, cannot, and should not establish day-to-day policy. What it can do is to react to and intervene on policies it deems inappropriate.[3]

Dewey responded to Lippmann with a book of his own, *The Public and Its Problems* (1927). Although it agreed with much of Lippmann's diagnosis, Dewey used this forum to present an alternative prognosis for democratic organization in the contemporary world.

Present practices, he admitted, fall short of democratic aspirations. The past is no longer a suitable guide. Just as the modern liberal view of freedom had assumed the universality of antecedently well-prepared individuals, so the older view of the public assumed "an omnicompetent citizen and the limitless capacity of public opinion" (LW 2:215). Such omnicompetence might have been more or less a reality in a society which, on the one hand, set severe limitations on who would actually count as citizens, and on the other, faced relatively more manageable social and technological issues. The assumption was not as easily defensible in a large, multi-ethnic, highly diversified nation faced with problems whose manageability required specialized expertise.

Contemporary democracies have more and more come to reject the social restrictions on citizenship common to the Greek *polis* and eighteenth-century America. The "public" is no longer a small ethnically homogeneous group who can automatically be assumed to support common moral, religious, and political ideals. When we add to this the multifaceted complexity of contemporary social issues, the estrangement of the public from the social/industrial experts who effectively make decisions is exacerbated. The public does seem to take on a ghostly, phantomlike aura. "Given such considerations, and the public and its organization for public ends is not only a ghost, but a ghost which walks and talks, and obscures, confuses and misleads governmental action in a disastrous way" (LW 2:313).

In this passage, Dewey agrees with the concerns of democratic realists. There is, to begin with, the fading away, the ghostliness, of a once vibrant, participatory force that was the public. Additionally, Dewey explicitly admits that when it has not receded into the background, when it does make itself felt, the public too often does so in an ill-conceived way.

The "public," Dewey is saying, too often does behave like a "mass." Ortega and the democratic realists have a point. What this represents for Dewey, however, is a challenge. Recognition of such limitations is helpful because it forces us to confront basic questions in relation to a living democracy:

What, after all, is the public under present conditions? What are the reasons for its eclipse? What hinders it from finding and identifying itself? By what means shall its inchoate and amorphous estate be organized into effective political action relevant to present social needs and opportunities? (LW 2:313)

As this quotation indicates, the conditions so well articulated by Lippmann, call, in Dewey's mind, for an effort to create a vibrant public. Just as neither freedom nor equality, in their fullness, could be said to pre-exist, so too the public is not a fixed antecedent reality. It is a result to be achieved.

To understand the depth of Dewey's concern, we must keep two things in mind. First, empirical naturalism pays as much attention to conditions and consequences as it does to the artic-ulation and comprehension of guiding ideals. Second, Dewey understands democracy to be an experiment-in-the making, not an already finished product in any of its contemporary incarna-tions.

Those who have chosen democracy have selected a chal-lenging course for themselves. If growth and individuality are to be fostered, then strenuous efforts based on actual conditions and arriving at concrete improvements will have to be undertaken. The "public," like freedom and equality, does not simply preexist in its fully perfect form, waiting to manifest itself once various obfuscating veils are removed. It is a product, a consequence dependent on the right mix of conditions. The challenge for those who would engage in the experiment of a democracy constantly in the making is to work at supplying those conditions.

The twentieth century provides too vivid examples of what can happen if democratic societies do not work well. Mussolini, for example, citing Ernest Renan's complaint that democracy "would be a social state in which a degenerate mass would have no other care than to enjoy the ignoble pleasures of vulgar men" (Cohen, 336), concluded that only a wholesale assault on liber-alism and democracy could provide conditions for a nobler human life. Dewey, always unflagging in his support of democ-racy, was nonetheless clear-eyed about its limitations and dan-gers. The Deweyan way of blunting the impact of future Mussolinis is to work at creating conditions wherein the *demos* will not be a "mass," but a genuine "public."

Ever the meliorist, Dewey sought to recognize deficiencies in order to overcome them, thereby strengthening democratic aspi-rations. Democracy, as we saw in the last chapter, involves more than the institutionalization of certain political practices. It is the social ideal which demands creative, experimental efforts to encourage freedom and equality understood as growth and indi-viduality. Basic to such an undertaking is the movement away from narrow preconceived or self-interested ends, to wider, more diversified, more community-centered ones. This sort of ideal highlights two dangerous forms of regression: (1) the eclipse of the public, and (2) its transformation into multiple self-interested groupings.

Problems of the Public

Following Lippmann's lead, Dewey took a hard look at present conditions. What resulted was an analysis identifying three contemporary tendencies toward the "mass" which had to be guarded against: (a) The public that is too narrow, (b) the public that is too diffuse, and (c) the public that is too distracted.

To judge these types of public as falling short of genuine democratic life requires from Dewey some criteria for identifying an exemplary public in a democratic community. He provides two such guidelines: "the degree of organization of the public which is attained and the degree in which its officers are so constituted as to perform their function of caring for public interest" (LW 2:256).

For a state to possess at least the formal requirement of democratic excellence these two factors must overlap. Its citizens must have a sense of being participants in the community's life. The public must be so organized that it can have a real impact on guiding public policy. In addition, the officials chosen to lead must recognize the full complexity of consequences that will result from important policy decisions. They must be sensitive to multiple social consequences, not merely whether narrow, sought-after ends will result.

Similar themes emerge from both criteria. There must be awareness of ideals, coupled with effective organization. Only then will a community utilize the energy necessary for establishing practices that are in line with the ideals. Without the ideals, the organization tends to translate into practices contrary to the society's well-being. Without the organization, ideals have little hope of becoming embodied in practice. Dewey's three distorted publics represent ways in which this combination of ideals and organization is not attained.

The Narrow Public

One drawback of present conditions is that there is no "public." It has been splintered into many narrowly self-interested publics. The impact on policy is that such publics, given opportunity and power, make unfortunate decisions with serious repercussions for the whole society. Dewey could allude to both prohibition and the Scopes trial as instances of public policy decisions which might be forthcoming from a narrowly focused, ill-informed citizenry. The prevalence of such policies encourages those who would denounce democracy. The antidemocratic alternative of a privileged ruling class which has special insight, and thus deserves to rule, is ever ready to rear its head.

> The attempt to decide by law that the legends of a primitive Hebrew people regarding the genesis of man are more authoritative than the results of scientific inquiry might be cited as a typical example of the sort of thing which is bound to happen when the accepted doctrine is that a public organized for political purposes, rather than experts guided by specialized inquiry, is the final umpire and arbiter of issues. (LW 2:313)

The first way, then, in which the ideals/organization symbiosis can be dissolved is when the various publics which comprise a society have splintered and balkanized themselves in such a way that no national public, sharing adherence to wider ideals, can be constituted. Narrow publics are overly devoted to self-interested goals which too often are either at variance with community ideals, or are forced upon the society as a whole.

The Diffuse Public

A second deviation from the democratic public derives from limitations of time, ability, and interest, combined with the expanding intricacy of contemporary issues. Such a public is too ill-informed and disorganized to have a serious impact on policy decisions.

> But the machine age has so enormously expanded, multiplied, intensified and complicated the scope of the indirect consequences, has formed such immense and consolidated unions in action, on an impersonal rather than a community basis, that the resultant public cannot identify and distinguish itself. (LW 2:314)

The Greek *polis* and Jefferson's agrarian democracy could take somewhat seriously the "omnicompetent" citizen. The conditions of contemporary society, however, make such "omnicompetence" more and more rare. "The problem of a democratically organized public is primarily and essentially an intellectual problem, in a degree to which the political affairs of prior ages offer no parallel" (LW 2:314).

What has replaced the public is a loose amalgam of citizens subject to the same legal code, and living within the country's geographical boundaries. They might have a vague perception of and allegiance to freedom and equality as shared ideals. However, when it comes to understanding contemporary issues and addressing them in light of these ideals their capabilities are limited.

To be a positive participatory force, a public has to apply democratic ideals to novel situations. We have already examined some of the difficulties surrounding the ideals of freedom and equality. The complexity of contemporary life compounds the problem. The inability to fathom important public issues, adequate housing, immigration, urban planning (to mention some addressed by Dewey), arms control, pollution, debtor nations, recalcitrant diseases (to name some newer ones), has more and more confused and diffused the public. Instead of being a powerful force promoting policies that implement the democratic promise, it is reduced to a shadow of its former self. It is loosely and vaguely held together by an allegiance to what have too often become detached, obscure ideals. Democratic practice then suffers a lack of vibrancy since its ideals are not fully manifested in the immensely complex situations of daily life.

The Distracted Public

In addition to the narrow and diffuse publics, Dewey signalled a third deviation: the distracted public. He quite readily admitted that democracy was based on "faith." He identified it as a "faith in the capacities of human nature; faith in human intelligence, and in the power of pooled cooperative experience" (LW 11:219). Such a faith is precarious and not widely held during the best of times. It becomes sorely strained when one acknowledges the dissipation of intellectual energy in an era of multiple distractions. "The members of an inchoate public have too many ways of enjoyment, as well as of work, to give much thought to organization into an effective public" (LW 2:321).

The increased pressures of career, coupled with the ever present allure of television, movies, radio, and the automobile, form an ineradicable part of contemporary existence. "That they did not originate in deliberate desire to divert attention from political interests does not lessen their effectiveness in that direction" (LW 2:321). For someone with Dewey's commitment to democracy it must have been disappointing to admit that "in most circles it is hard work to sustain conversation on a political theme; and once initiated, it is quickly dismissed with a yawn" (LW 2:321). Democratic faith in human nature and its intelligence is sorely tested when such hard work is compared to the relative ease with which individuals will sustain a discussion about the "mechanism and accomplishment of various makes of motor cars or the respective merits of actresses" (LW 2:322).

An Ezra Pound, a Giovanni Gentile, or a Mussolini, surveying the intellectual territory thus mapped out by Dewey would be quick to offer a solution: reject democracy as a misguided and unworkable ideal. The people are really the "masses" and must be guided by an enlightened leader. Dewey, by contrast, neither despairs nor offers radical panaceas meant to resolve democracy's shortcomings at a single stroke. His reaction rather divides into two parts: (1) He offers a reconstructed democratic theory free from the limitations linked to modernity. (2) He makes specific suggestions about the factors to be addressed if the public necessary to a democratic community is to revive itself. The first of these was examined in the previous chapter. The second is the subject being presently discussed.

Conditions for Reviving the Public

"Practical democracy" was how Dewey entitled his review of Lippmann's *The Phantom Public*. Such a title reveals Dewey's sensitivity to the Madison-type concerns about "pure" democracy. The title also embodies Dewey's fondest hope: to give flesh and bones to democratic theory, making it a vibrant presence in human practice. Philosophy, "criticism" in the Deweyan sense, is a means to help further the arrival of a healthy democracy. Lippmann too, according to Dewey, did not undertake a critique in order to turn his back on democratic aspirations. Rather, Lippmann's criticism could be read as

> a statement of faith in a pruned and temperate democratic theory, and a presentation of methods by which a reasonable conception of democracy can be made to work, not

absolutely, but at least better than democracy works under an exaggerated and undisciplined notion of the public and its powers. (LW 2:213)

Dewey's description of Lippmann's aim could just as easily have been a self-description. He too sought to foster conditions within which a "reasonable conception of democracy can be made to work."

The philosopher's task is that of supplying the intellectual grid within which democratic life will have a realistic opportunity for thriving. In Deweyan language, the fundamental challenge is that of providing a ground map which will allow the transformation from a "Great Society" to a "Great Community."

"Great Society" was a label taken from the title of an influential book published in 1914 by Graham Wallas. By using the expression, Wallas sought to indicate the novel environment that had been fashioned by historical and technological changes. This was the environment that made large, geographically dispersed nations possible. It also seemed to present a milieu beyond the control of ordinary citizens. The factors influencing an individual life are distant, highly specialized, and under the control of a class of bureaucrats or technicians. The presence of such a complex, technologically advanced culture, occasions the need to rethink the role of the public. How can demo-cracy, power in the hands of the public, be translated into effective practice within the Great Society?

Dewey's response is to attempt an articulation of the conditions which would foster a vibrant, participatory, full-blooded public. He is not so naive as to imagine that such an ideal will ever be attained absolutely. We have already seen how he is sensitive to the failings of the public. He is concerned, however, that this remain the ideal which guides the formative, ongoing experiment known as democracy. Such an ideal has at least the advantage of imposing the right set of responsibilities on the citizenry. But, if the Great Society fosters the splintering of the public, its diffusion and its distraction, how can its reconstitution be accomplished?

There is one term which, for Dewey, aligns the various factors he would bring to bear on democratic life. That term is "communication." This is a word which bears much (some might say too much) weight in Dewey's analyses. In order to grasp its meaning, we have to understand it principally in its etymological sense. "Communication" suggests the process of becoming more unified. The whole cluster of activities involved in encouraging solidarity are encompassed in the Deweyan usage. It does not refer to any single mode or manner of social intercourse. What it does indicate is a multifaceted harmonizing process.

> There is more than a verbal tie between the words common, community, and communication. Men live in a community in virtue of the things which they have in common; and communication is the way in which they come to possess things in common. What they must have in common in order to form a community or society are aims, beliefs, aspirations, knowledge—a common understanding—likemindedness as the sociologists say. (MW 9:7)

The kind of "like-mindedness" which is prerequisite for a community is no longer an inheritance that can be taken for granted. More cohesive societies like Winthrop's could build from a shared set of beliefs, aspirations, and experiences. For complex contemporary societies this like-mindedness is a result to be achieved not a preexistent given to be assumed. Because of this, communication plays a special role in Dewey's reconstruction of democratic theory.

The "communication" Dewey has in mind is one that will insure "participation in a common understanding," one which "secures similar emotional and intellectual dispositions—like ways of responding to expectations and requirements" (MW 9:7). Such an ideal of fostering what is in effect national character, habitual dispositions to act and respond in particular ways, is what guides Deweyan thinking with regard to democratic life. Absent some form of "like-mindedness," a large population within fixed geographic boundaries remains an agglomeration. It has not been transformed into a community.

The question to be addressed is whether Dewey's optimism has gotten the best of him here. If democracy were viewed as something more than an experiment, if it were thought of as a fixed and final social arrangement, rather than as a constantly burgeoning process, this might well be the case. Dewey's Great Community will never be perfectly realized. What its projection as an ideal does, though, is to channel effort and responsibility in a particular direction. Naive optimism may indeed be out of the question, but a realistic hope is not.

By focusing on communication, Dewey carves out a channel to guide human energies. Specifically, Dewey challenges the democratic citizenry in three ways:

1. They must revise the outdated symbolism which promotes a value system more consistent with the past than with the present.
2. The "experimental method," the method of intelligence in operation described in chapter 2, must be brought to bear on social and political concerns.
3. The process of gathering and disseminating news must be recognized as an art, and reformed in light of artistic values.

The Need for New Symbols

If the ideals of a Great Community are to be shared, they first have to be understood. We have seen in the previous chapter how democratic ideals need to be disassociated from the individualistic assumptions that were prevalent in Modern philosophy. Those assumptions, when absorbed into practice, tend to encourage the splintering of community and the fostering of agglomeration. By the twentieth century those assumptions have so permeated public life that they are embodied in images that encourage those misleading ideals even further.

Whether on magazine covers, in the text of advertisements, in political sloganeering, or in the discourse of television talk shows, the symbols inherited from modernity are ubiquitous. Wealth, celebrity, self-interest, autonomy, power, youth, present themselves in various ways as indices which have preeminence in our culture. They are viewed as automatically honorific, engaging the attention and allegiance of those exposed to them. No serious changes will take place until new symbols become prominent. "Symbols control sentiment and thought, and the new age has no symbols consistent with its activities" (LW 2:323).

The symbolic embodiments which have dominated our existence in the twentieth century form a consistent inheritance. They range from the detective Philip Marlowe, the solitary western hero Shane, the celebrations of self-indulgence in popular television programs, to the lionizing of wealthy executives. These figures, whether actual or fictional, stand both as reflections of a particular ideal of human life and as incitements to pursue that ideal. What unites them is the assumption of individualism rather than individuality. They are depicted in a way that isolates them from family connections, social relations, and cultural heritage. They set fixed goals, and are not fastidious about the means for achieving them. They tend to go their own way, and are critical if not outright hostile to the more complex and messy processes involved in dealing with public officials and agencies. They set things aright according to their own view of what needs to be done.

Alternative symbols, the father who does not make a mark in the world of wealth but who cares deeply for his children and raises them well, the schoolteacher who must forge incipient communities year after year, the family farming the same land for generations, the PTA volunteer, all of those individuals who might embody ideals of sharing, of the common good, of self-effacement, of caring for others, of cooperation, are present but eclipsed by these other more prominent symbols. Words like "attachment" or "connection," as we have seen in the previous chapter, are more likely the conjure up restrictive connotations than those of working together to gain greater capacity for implementing social goods.

In several recent works, Robert Bellah and his associates have begun the retrieval of alternative symbolisms. They have pointed out that America's heritage is rich beyond the utilitarian individualism which has been dominant since the nineteenth century. Earlier traditions which they identify as the "biblical" (associated with the Puritan notion of commonwealth) and "republican" (associated with the Jeffersonian ideal of participatory citizenship), need to be restored to their proper place in the country's communal consciousness (Bellah, 1986, 28–32).

The work thus begun will only have a real impact if it is given embodiment in the popular arts. These latter are not, for Dewey, neutral factors in community life. A living, effective public cannot be brought into existence unless the intellectual and artistic communities create new symbols. These will have to be appropriate to an altered, more community-sensitive interpretation of democracy.

Intelligence in Operation

An attempt to reform the symbols which dominate our life is only one of the ingredients needed for reviving the public. It can help focus on genuinely democratic ideals, but it must be accompanied by a reform in the way people reflect and deliberate. What

Dewey calls the "experimental method" or "social intelligence" or "intelligence in operation" defines a sort of activity that needs to become habitual in democratic communities. Democratic principles worked out in practice by nondemocratic means of deliberation present a blueprint for a truncated, frustrated democracy.

The central concerns for citizens in a democracy are analogous to those of a jurist who must determine how law and precedent apply to present, often novel, situations. The democratic public and its officials must deal with issues of immediate concern in light of guiding ideals. Such a task, given improper epistemological assumptions, could too easily translate into an absolutist political agenda. If the question of truth reduces simply to the need of a mind to grasp definitively an already existing solution, then self-satisfaction, professions of certainty, and the temptation to authoritarianism are likely results. Empirical naturalism, as we have already seen, offers an alternative: social intelligence engaged in the responsibility of criticism.

Political inquiry is not to be thought of on the model of a "mind" examining "ideas," "concepts," or even "external" objects. Prevailing theories of knowledge, which consider reflection as direct analysis of concepts, channel intellectual energy into unproductive areas. Certain "problems" are invented as the result of erroneous philosophical assumptions. Concepts like "authority" are opposed to the concept "freedom." The idea of "personal rights" is examined in contrast to its foil, "social obligations." This is philosophical sport, analyses of concepts which, in their abstract purity, can be set down as incompatible polarities. Such philosophical play, however, provides only "subsumptive illustrative reference to empirical facts."

What is needed for the fruitful thinking through of political issues is rather inquiry into "the *consequences* of some particular distribution, under given conditions, of specific freedoms and authorities, and for inquiry into what altered distribution would yield more desirable consequences" (LW 2:356). The Galilean Purification would have us isolate concepts in their purity so that they may be more amenable to that philosophical play known as conceptual analysis. In place of this, empirical naturalism urges an exploration of how actual practices, almost always hybrid manifestations of the pure, separate concepts, play themselves out in practice. These consequences can then be examined to determine whether they further or inhibit democratic aspirations.

Dewey is here mounting a forceful challenge to a standard mode of procedure in philosophy. Philosophers have often thought of their role as that of analyzing concepts. What Dewey points out is the sterility of such approaches. A philosopher interested in art, for example, could examine the concepts "useful" and "beautiful" and then come to the conclusion that the two are wholly incompatible. The idea "useful" is not beautiful, nor does the idea "beautiful" contain any trace of utility. Yet actual observation of the world about us reveals that, though the two ideas exclude each other, their intermixture or hybridization is a fact of life.

Rejecting the picture of the philosopher who withdraws for the purpose of analyzing ideas, Dewey prefers the example of an artist engaged in fabrication as more accurately symbolizing the process of deliberation. Shaker artisans, for example, were not concerned with the relation of the concept "beautiful" to the concept "useful." Rather they examined the consequences of working with various woods, designs, and shapes in light of particular functions. Not worrying about the incompatibility of rival concepts, they could produce chairs and tables that embodied both beauty and utility.

The sorts of questions asked by artists, and the experiments they carry out, represent the model of inquiry that Dewey believes is an essential component of the communication he deems necessary to democratic life. Democratic ideals may be inherited. Allegiance to them may be assumed automatically among certain peoples. Nonetheless, if these are to be more than honorific phantoms themselves, the public must give them life in daily practice. Social inquiry carried on under the rubric of intelligence in action can encourage that project.

The focus of attention, as Dewey indicates, is that of determining what results will occur as outcomes of different associated activities. Which institutions and conditions, when properly guided, will forge the means for best realizing democratic ideals? What are the actual consequences of certain patterns of associated activities? Will they maximize opportunities for the all-round growth, multifaceted participation, and effective freedom as capability that should be the hallmarks of democratic life?

Processes of this sort cannot be accomplished by the isolated thinker seeking direct insight into ideas. They are the product of people working together, gathering information, projecting hypothetically, listening to experts, and debating positions. It is messy, frustrating, too often ill-fated work. But it may be the best we have. It is certainly the method of intelligence most con-

ducive to democratic practice. Without widespread acknowledgment that social intelligence, not direct confrontation with and
insight into truths, is the most appropriate human mode of coming to warranted assertions, the chances of creating a community
are, as far as Dewey is concerned, slim.

The overarching interest of empirical naturalism is always
concern with the good. In political discourse this translates into a
concern for the well-being of citizens. Such a concern is important
because it is coordinated with an attitude toward political theory
which rejects *a priori* commitments to intellectual schemes.
"Criticism," as we have seen, examines conditions and consequences. The proper beginning for social and political philosophy is neither with a commitment to ideological purity nor to an
antecedently determined political structure which must be maintained whatever the consequences. Idolatry of fixed antecedent
ideological conclusions or institutions (e.g., no private ownership
of the means of production) too easily results in a situation where
purity of theory is preferred over the well-being of citizens.

Whereas philosophers in the past have tended toward
world-historical pronouncements, grandiose readings of history,
or fixed allegiance to absolute foundational certainties, Dewey
suggests the more modest procedure of social intelligence. Like
genuine freedom and equality, this intelligence is a product to be
cultivated, not something with a full-blown antecedent existence.
Democratic citizens would be misleading themselves if they
believed that free inquiry as social intelligence simply appears
when censorship is abolished. The absence of censorship is an
occasion for free inquiry not a sufficient condition for it.

> The belief that thought and its communication are now free
> simply because legal restrictions which once obtained have
> been done away with is absurd. . . . Removal of formal lim-
> itations is but a negative condition; positive freedom is not a
> state but an act which involves methods and instrumental-
> ities for control of conditions. . . . But a belief in intellectual
> freedom where it does not exist contributes only to com-
> placency in virtual enslavement, to sloppiness, superficial-
> ity and recourse to sensations as a substitute for ideas:
> marked traits of our present estate with respect to social
> knowledge. (LW 2:340)

The older epistemology, positing a "mind" confronting
"ideas" directly, could consider the absence of restraints pro-

hibiting such confrontation as synonymous with free inquiry. The latter, within such a scheme, could be attained as soon as the evils of these restraints were removed. But the situation here is analogous to that of effective freedom discussed in the previous chapter. Dewey thinks that so long as we are guided by out-dated beliefs, democratic aspirations will be retarded rather than advanced. Community will be engendered when the participatory, tentative, experimental character of intelligence in action comes to be recognized as the proper approach to social inquiry. This approach, however, is not simply lying there, antecedently given and ready to spring forth complete and perfect when restraints are removed.

Like any healthy activity it needs to be exercised in order to be both developed and maintained. The dominant epistemology frustrates this development by ignoring what is really needed: conceptions which "are used as tools of directed inquiry and which are tested, rectified and caused to grow in actual use" (LW 2:340).

Concepts, ideas, even ideals are never ends in themselves for Dewey. Consummatory experiences which both embody and enhance the well-being of individuals are the only ends-in-them-selves. Social intelligence is the shared process of determining the direction practice should take. This kind of intelligence can-not claim to have achieved direct, full intuition of truth. What it can do is continue the process of criticism and suggestion. The consummatory phase of experience will then have a greater prevalence than it does now.

> Democracy will come into its own, for democracy is a name for a life of free and enriching communion. It had its seer in Walt Whitman. It will have its consummation when free social inquiry is indissolubly wedded to the art of full and moving communication. (LW 2:350)

Communication may be imperfect. It may never attain the status that Dewey projects for it. Yet, it remains a worthy ideal and a preferred substitute for its alternative, a society forged by "force" (LW 2:332).

Public Media

Social intelligence and appropriate symbols are two ingre-dients that go into the activity of communication. They would, however, remain isolated unless they were allied to an effective means of disseminating information. As in the cases of freedom, equality, and genuine social inquiry, removal of legal restrictions does not by itself signal the presence of an effective press. Indeed, the absence of control brings with it a new set of concerns. "But when we ask what sort of material is recorded and how it is organized, when we ask about the intellectual form in which the material is presented, the tale to be told is very different" (LW 2:347).

Revising one's assumptions is a process that involves automatic spillover into other areas. The need to develop a social intelligence may not be recognized. In many ways the public demands of social intelligence are difficult. How much easier is it for academics to bury themselves in arcana and speak a dialect incomprehensible to all but the initiated. How much easier for those charged with news gathering is the process of simply repeating information given to them (in news conferences, briefings, press releases), commenting on the lives of celebrities, or commissioning public opinion surveys, rather than telling the story adequately. Social intelligence requires the examination of conditions and consequences. News reports that can barely get beyond the headline or focus on visuals rather than information are minimally helpful for a democratic public. Information media then become an easy tool for manipulation by those in power.

What is called "news" involves mostly irruptions of striking events which seem to occur without context, history, or even consequences, since these are rarely followed out. News comes to be thought of as what intrudes on the daily course of events. Without a narrative which connects conditions and consequences, events appear simply as sorts of spontaneous generations. So long as the news is defined narrowly as the "new" in this sense, no lasting, properly functioning participatory public will be possible. The *meaning* of news "depends upon relation to what it imports, to what its social consequences are." This sort of significance cannot "be determined unless the new is placed in relation to the old, to what has happened and been integrated into the course of events" (LW 2:347).

Stating accurately what has been said at a news conference or presented at a briefing may represent the acme of "objective" reporting. "Objectivity" may also be guaranteed in a report that states the who, what, where, and when of a social disturbance. This sort of objectivity depends on the subject/object distinction prominent in traditional empiricism. The subject is defined primarily as a spectator listing the facts which are given. But such a model is insufficient when it comes to telling the whole story. The news story needs to be understood on analogy with its literary counterpart. The story is always situated in a historical context, results from a variety of factors, and is significant only in such terms.

Such telling of a story is, however, difficult work. It is difficult because the events are complicated and the audience diverse. Not only is the audience diverse, but too often "the mass of the reading public is not interested in learning and assimilating the results of accurate investigation" (LW 2:349). The way to overcome these difficulties involves the proper manner of crafting the narrative, in a word, "art." "Presentation is fundamentally important, and presentation is a question of art." An educated public might demand the kind of thorough treatment of issues provided by in-depth studies. Realistically, however, a "newspaper which was only a daily edition of a quarterly journal of sociology or political science would undoubtedly possess a limited circulation and a narrow influence."

Journalists have a very special role to play in Dewey's version of a democratic republic. They can rise to this role if they foster the talent of writing that is both thorough yet accessible to a wide audience. Admittedly, this is a difficult challenge. Nonetheless, "the freeing of the artist in literary presentation . . . is as much a precondition of the desirable creation of adequate opinion on public matters as is the freeing of social inquiry" (LW 2:349).

Against this Deweyan ideal must be contrasted the realities that confront news organizations. They are limited in personnel, dependent on popularity for success and funding, devoted to notions of "objectivity" and news selection that are allied to past epistemologies. Journalists too often see themselves as neutral, disinterested spectators, simply mirroring events. Such a picture is modelled on modernity's "spectator theory of knowledge" which Dewey worked so hard at dislodging. At the very least, journalists should realize that, far from being "objective," they make value judgments the moment they decide which stories to tell, the sequence in which they relate them, and the amount of time/space allotted to each.

Journalists are widely recognized as crucial to the success of democracy. Limitations in theory and resources, however, hamper the role they could play. No effective public can be built on the rigid division between a class of experts speaking to each other in technical journals and the great majority of citizens exposed to a daily digest of "crime, accident, family rows, personal clashes and conflicts" (LW 2:347).

An Effective Public

An effective public will be one engaged in an ongoing discourse about both general ideals and contemporary concerns. The circuitry of intelligence in action involves various components:

1. Awareness of fundamental principles
2. Attention to consequences of varied actions
3. Information about contemporary issues
4. Dissemination of the results of social inquiry
5. Transforming all of this into instrumentalities for social change.

The entire circuitry is important because democracy is a form of association constantly in the making. Complacency, the belief that any particular set of institutions and laws has finally established perfect democracy, is an enemy of democratic life. What results from such complacency is a lowering of effort at enhancing social well-being. The belief that democracy is once and for all in place is a powerful temptation to relax our efforts, to excuse deficiencies, and to ignore the Deweyan challenge of looking always at conditions and consequences. What remains, too often, is simply the belief that democratic life is merely the creation of a society that allows the self-interested pursuits of wealth and power.

Dewey believed that the establishment of a genuinely democratic life would be difficult. His concern was always that the citizens of a society be provided with the appropriate conditions for personal growth and community participation. Such an ideal always looks to actual situations. It examines established laws and institutions in light of this ideal. Because of this attitude, Dewey could not make the sort of absolutist, atemporal pronouncements of which philosophers are too often fond. Dewey will not be found, for example, asserting as dogma that oppression of the working class will end as soon as private ownership of the means of production is abolished. Nor will he be found claiming that the roles of the state are limited to protection from external threat and provision for internal order.

What he can do is to articulate the modifications in theory that accrue with empirical naturalism. This is followed by concrete suggestions toward the furthering of democratic aspirations. We might well claim that Dewey was overly optimistic, that half a century later we are no nearer the realization of democratic life. Still he hoped that his suggestions of a piecemeal tinkering for improvement offered a better course to follow than more high-sounding but also more dangerously antidemocratic alternatives. The citizens can tend toward the "mass" or they can tend toward the "public." Dewey's political philosophy seeks to articulate the conditions appropriate for encouraging the latter.

5

Educating

A Simple Credo

When John Dewey entered the Burlington, Vermont school system he found himself in a class that was large, there were fifty-four students, and heterogeneous, their ages ranged from 7 to 19. This was in 1867, a time when efforts to improve American schools were already under way. The following year, thanks to the efforts of reformers, Dewey found himself in a more central-ized system. The newer system aimed at citywide standards of conformity, a centerpiece of which was the sorting out of stu-dents into classes consistent with age. Nonetheless, studies pre-pared at this time indicate the limitations still inherent in edu-cational practice. One such report revealed that, for most students, learning was identified with exercises of repetition and memorization, a "lifeless, monotonous droning of syllables" (Dykhuizen, 187). A widely repeated slogan of the time claimed that "it makes no difference what you teach a boy so long as he doesn't like it" (MW 9:141).

By the end of his life, eighty-five years later, Dewey had wit-nessed drastic changes in the educational system. Although the changes effected under the name of "progressive education" were not all consistent with his views,[1] his role as a central figure in the task of rethinking the nature of education in a democratic society was widely celebrated. That role was guided by a simple credo: "What the best and wisest parent wants for his own child, that must the community want for all of its children" (MW 1:5).

This chapter will attempt to explain the philosophical land-scape within which Dewey cultivated the fruits of his sugges-tions for ameliorating the American educational system. These suggestions, as we will see, are far from being radical. Dewey was surprisingly old-fashioned. This is not to say that he was conservative, if "conservative" means a desire to preserve the status quo. He worked hard at revising established educational practices.

To say that he was old-fashioned is to indicate that his model of education was a traditional kind of formation: the kind that children would have gotten in the home or on the farm. The whole challenge of Deweyan educational philosophy involves the attempt to preserve the best of home education in a world where schooling as a distinct institution had become a necessity.

A home is a place where a child's curiosity is stimulated as a result of conversation and of projects carried out. Sharing in family work helps occasion habits such as cooperation, industry, and dependability. It also provides an initial context within which problems need to be solved by research and experimentation. In addition, the family serves as a springboard from which the child interacts with others, and through which the wider cultural and natural worlds are introduced.

> Now if we organize and generalize all of this, we have the ideal school. There is no mystery about it, no wonderful discovery of pedagogy or educational theory. It is simply a question of doing systematically and in a large, intelligent, and competent way what for various reasons can be done in most households only in a comparatively meager and haphazard manner. (MW 1:23–24)

What we need to keep in mind about Dewey, then, is that he is old-fashioned without being conservative. He does not accept the continuation of ongoing practices. But the modifications to be pursued are motivated by traditionalist considerations. The greatest appeal of the home is the integrative nature of the formation that children there receive. Intellect, emotion, affection, manual skill, and moral development are woven together in the child's upbringing. Such an integrative approach runs counter, Dewey realizes, to the philosophical assumptions prominent in the West since the seventeenth century. As a philosopher, his efforts at reform go hand in hand with the reconstruction of those assumptions as described in the previous chapters.

Two branches of philosophy are particularly significant with regard to education: philosophical anthropology and political philosophy. From early in his career, Dewey took notice of the fact that any theory of education was part of a philosophical outlook which adopted, whether consciously or unconsciously, a particular understanding of human nature. If Locke, Rousseau, Herbart, and Pestalozzi offered differing proposals for education, this was due, in great part, to their diverging philosophical anthropologies. Making explicit his own understanding of the human condition thus became a central task for Dewey.

In addition, Dewey was sensitive to the perspective, as ancient as Aristotle and Plato, that a theory of education is linked irrecusably to the sort of political system within which it is exercised. A philosophy of education must keep one eye focused on philosophical anthropology to understand the possibilities and limitations of human beings. The other must focus on the political system which sets the general goals of education. "The conception of education as a social process and function has no definite meaning until we define the kind of society we have in mind" (MW 9:103).

My own analysis will divide along these two paths of philosophical anthropology and political philosophy. The first path will follow Dewey's rejection of his great *bete noire*, dualism, and its accompanying asomatic attitude. By moving beyond dualism, Dewey introduces a reevaluation of the body, and a redefinition of "mind." Several important Deweyan themes emerge in this connection.

1. Dewey makes an important distinction between a narrowly "vocational" education, and one that is built around what he calls "occupations." "Occupations" are made central, while narrow vocationalism is rejected outright.
2. Education is not preparation. Education, for Dewey, is important only so far as it is treated as an end in itself. Education treated as preparation for external and future ends represents one great failing of traditional pedagogical methods.

The second path follows Dewey's understanding of "democracy." This is a topic that continues the discussion of the previous two chapters. As we have seen, Dewey significantly altered ordinary conceptions of democracy. He planted the seeds for a wider understanding of democracy as a "way of life" built around the centrality of growth and individuality.

His reconceptualization of democracy led him to recommend that an educational system must encourage certain habits while it discourages others. The Deweyan suggestions go beyond the traditional claim that education's goal in a democratic society must be to produce an informed electorate. The inculcation of a democratic character, not just the training of citizens' minds, is that toward which an educational system in a democracy must aim. The question of moral education thus becomes a focal concern.

Beyond Modern Man

Empirical naturalism carved out its identity in opposition to the dualistic heritage rooted in Descartes. Dewey was especially vigorous in carrying out a veritable crusade against the post-Cartesian imposition of a vision he considered both artificial and false. This is the position I will identify as that of "Modern man" (masculine used advisedly). How can "Modern man" be characterized? First, we need to identify two great bifurcations which circumscribe this interpretation of the human condition. One is internal, the other external. Internally, Modern man considers himself to be composed of two substances, mind (*res cogitans*) and body (*res extensa*). Externally, Modern man views himself as a "subject" separate from and confronting a world considered as "external." This external world is composed of "objects."

The epistemology which arises from these bifurcations, as we have seen in chapter two, Dewey calls the "spectator theory of knowledge." This epistemology considers man as if he were a spectator at the theater. He is a "subject" separated from the world's "objects." Modern man's aim was a kind of knowledge consistent with this spectator stance. The prototypical activities of the spectator are seeing and listening. The two senses of sight and hearing, those which can most readily be disassociated from the body, become the privileged pathways for human cognition.

When the body/mind dualism is linked to the priority of sight and hearing, the optimal epistemological situation is characterized by traits which have significant implications for an educational system: (1) detachment, (2) objectivity, and (3) passivity. Man as spectator is someone who can rise above the hustle and bustle of daily life to become a purely receptive viewer and listener taking in objective data.

To understand Dewey properly we have to emphasize how he replaces the Cartesian asomatic prototype with a post-Darwinian, embodied one. The human condition is not one of being bifurcated. It is, rather, that of being a concrete living being in a living world. Such a creature is not at all a pure "mind" whose primary concern is to grasp eternal truths. The creature is rather a human being concerned with securing an optimal mode of existence as a sociocultural being.

The central elements of the Deweyan anthropology can be summarized in the following two-pronged way: First, the asomatic attitude is rejected. Embodiedness together with bodily activity are understood to be integral factors of the human condition. Within a dualistic anthropology, the body is thought of as an annoyance or as that which interferes with the purer, higher work of mind. By contrast, post-Darwinian anthropology recognizes bodily activity as a necessary component in human cognition. Without it, knowing would be impoverished. The models here are those of scientists such as Louis Pasteur and Claude Bernard. Their work required hands-on experimentation. The models are no longer the Rodin-type thinker, isolated and withdrawn, seeking to contemplate eternal truths by means of a mind that is as detached from the body as possible.

Second, the community becomes focal. Interaction and sociality, as we have seen, are inextricable accompaniments of human life. Since individuals always find themselves linked with others in a community, the search for truth is best conducted as a joint project. The thinker, sitting alone and contemplating, must be replaced by a community of inquirers who share in the task of uncovering, creating, and articulating truths.

These two prongs had been largely marginalized by postmedieval philosophy. Modern man's self-understanding brought with it certain implications for education. The most important was the manner in which "mind" was understood. When vision and hearing are privileged, "mind" becomes a sort of interior eye or ear which works separately from the body. Its goal becomes the direct apprehension of pure truth, objective and universal. "Mind" is thought of as a fixed and completed faculty whose capacity can be activated by simply taking its place as a spectator in the theater of life. It can then perceive truths about the world. "Mind" begins as an empty container. Schooling is the process of filling it with appropriate content.

When, however, we situate "mind" within a context free from the Asomatic Attitude, a richer set of meanings emerges. "Mind" should, first of all, be treated more as a verb than as a substantive. It "denotes all the ways in which we deal consciously and expressly with the situations in which we find ourselves" (LW

10:268). Dewey, as is typical for him, looks to ordinary usage rather than to specialized philosophical contexts, for exploring more generous meanings for "mind." Those, he claims, do not reflect the sharp separation of mind from body. "For in its non-technical use, 'mind' denotes every mode and variety of interest in, and concern for, things: practical, intellectual, and emotional" (LW 10:267–68). Children are told to "mind" their parents. An individual has a "mind" to engage in some project. We are re-"minded" of past events. A father "minds" his children, and a tourist in Britain must "mind" low archways. This combination of colloquial uses bespeaks a term signifying a cluster of activities, not a passive container. In addition, the highlighted activities do not make sharp distinctions between the mental and the bodily. "In short, 'to mind' denotes an activity that is intellectual, to *note* something; affectional, as caring and liking, and volitional, prac-tical, acting in a purposive way" (LW 10:267).

Once again, the home setting presents a model to be fol-lowed. In the family, the child is treated as a unified being whose affective, intellectual, and motor capabilities are developed in a harmonious fashion. "Mind" is not thought of as something opposed to the body, but rather as the full working out of the child's capacities.

Occupations

Transferring this model to the school means that educa-tion will have to focus on what Dewey calls "occupations." This was a term which caused much misunderstanding of Dewey's position. He was thought to be suggesting narrow vocational-ism, "pragmatic" training so that students could be well shaped for the jobs that awaited them. But nothing could be further from the truth. Dewey resisted strenuously any attempt to trans-form education into vocational training. The latter, he believed, would aggravate class differences by sorting out students into the privileged who received a liberal education, and the lower classes, trained only for a particular task.

This sort of system is better suited for an aristocratic society than for a democratic one. It simply duplicates on the social scale the bifurcation thought to define human life: a higher, cul-tured class representing "mind," a lower, working class repre-senting "body."

While training for the profession of learning is regarded as the type of culture, or a liberal education, the training of a mechanic, a musician, a lawyer, a doctor, a farmer, a merchant, or a railroad manager is regarded as purely technical and professional. The result is that which we see about us everywhere—the division into "cultured" people and "workers," the separation of theory and practice. (MW 1:18)

Traditional schooling, organized within the Asomatic Attitude, thus reveals two serious limitations.

1. Its practice creates an artificial, spectator-type, environment based on a faulty view of human nature.
2. It runs counter to the ideals of a democratic society.

Dewey's response is to offer a proposal which treats the child as an integrated individual. What counts is that the educational process be so construed that what the child learns will be most fully and effectively absorbed. The traditional classroom is constructed on a two-pronged assumption:

1. Mind as an empty container waiting to be filled with cultural content, and
2. Body as a machine waiting to be customized for a particular function.

Dewey begins with an alternative conception of human nature: that of a psychosomatic unity, a child with native impulses and interests whose formation must be consistent with its active and inquisitive nature. He goes so far as to claim that under the present system of schooling, children must leave behind their minds (in the active Deweyan understanding of this term) as they enter the classroom.

If he had a purely abstract mind, he could bring it to school with him, but his is a concrete one, interested in concrete things, and unless these things get over into school life, he cannot take his mind with him. What we want is to have the child come to school with a whole mind and a whole body, and leave school with a fuller mind and an even healthier body. (MW 1:49–50)

The activity around which schooling would best carry out this formation is what Dewey calls "occupation." "Occupation" here does not mean a job or even training for a particular kind of work. It means, rather, an enterprise which marshals energy for the accomplishment of a goal. Sewing, building, gardening, and cooking are all examples of occupations. An occupation is an activity which "reproduces, or runs parallel to, some form of work carried on in social life." An occupation maintains "a balance between the intellectual and practical phase in experience."

The centrality of occupations in schooling does not derive from the desire to prepare for a particular career. "Occupation as thus conceived must, therefore, be carefully distinguished from work which educates primarily for a trade" (MW 1:92). What Dewey wishes to do is create a context in which what is learned will be integrated into a student's experiences. This will optimize the opportunities for recognizing the importance of studies, and of absorbing them. Abstract lessons, rote memorization, lists of dates or chemical compounds, might be the suitable ingredients for a mind which is a container needing to be filled. They are not the most suitable pedagogical methodology for children needing the best sort of formation.

Any system of schooling must build on a child's natural curiosity and interests. It must also recognize that the child is fundamentally an active participant, not a passive spectator. Schooling in which occupations are central does just this. An occupation, say gardening, is not made focal in order to prepare the future gardeners of the world. "It affords an avenue of approach to knowledge of the place farming and horticulture have had in the history of the race and which they occupy in present social organization" (MW 9:208). Occupations offer an opportune context within which schooling can succeed because they allow the child's natural curiosity to be channelled in the direction of more specialized work. The continuities between the fundamental needs and activities of life and the refined researches of advanced disciplines is thereby highlighted.

Cooking is another example provided by Dewey. The importance of kitchens in the schools is not to prepare professional chefs. What a kitchen does is offer the opportunity to associate an ordinary activity of life with a variety of interests that develop into specialized disciplines. The need for food and the practices of its preparation provide a special pedagogical opportunity for expanding the interests of the children and stimulating their curiosity. Questions about the sources of food lead immediately to questions about the natural world. Geographical and meteorological considerations can be introduced in this context. The cultivation of food as well as its cooking, can serve as ways of introducing biological and chemical considerations. Socially, the issues raised by a discussion centered on food can make more concrete the causes of revolutions, the need for political economy, and the importance of commerce.[2]

An education built around "occupations" thus allows educators to draw on natural interests in the hope of building genuine curiosity about intellectual matters. Education then proceeds in widening concentric circles around the center of occupations. The aim is always that of reaching as many students as possible, and reaching them in the most effective manner. The traditional subjects are not neglected, nor is the necessarily more formal, abstract work associated with advanced levels of instruction, minimized. But in each case, the continuities with ordinary life activities are recognized rather than ruptured.

In his report to the president of the University of Chicago on the experimental school that came to bear his name, Dewey articulated the main rings of the concentric circles that make up an educational experience centered on occupations. The first ring involves identifying the interests of the students "in order to select subject-matter and methods with the greatest probability of calling the whole child into activity at each stage." The second is the task of properly organizing subject-matter. The aim of such organization is the cumulative building on what has come before. The third circle incorporates the beginning of specialization. At this stage the student is introduced to the "gradual distinction of the subject-matter into its more specialized phases." The final circle of activity is that of introducing more formal methods, abstract thinking, working with symbols, and working more exclusively with textbooks. The challenge here is to "provide demand and opportunity for the continuous introduction of symbols in reading, writing, and number, and the necessity for an increased use of books as auxiliaries" (MW 1:319).

The traditional classroom was perfectly organized for minds-as-containers to receive the information deemed necessary by school authorities. There was, to begin with, a clean separation between the world outside of the school and the activities in the school. The classroom was organized for optimal spectatorial success: fixed desks facing a professor who was, in effect, on stage. The full impact of the traditional organization struck Dewey as he sought out appropriate furniture for the laboratory school's classrooms. After explaining his needs to a supplier, the latter responded tellingly "you want something at which the children may work; these are all for listening" (MW 1:21).

If the post-Darwinian understanding of humans were accepted, such a physical setting would have to be changed. The classroom, according to Dewey, must become a center for doing. It must be a place where students can engage in activities and experiments. Both bodily and mental dimensions of the students must be challenged. To incorporate such a change, it would be necessary to eliminate the fixed rows of desks best suited for listening and rote repetition. Classrooms, as traditionally designed, "are hostile to the existence of real situations of experience." They are too far removed from the "conditions of everyday life which will generate difficulties." Such settings overemphasize "listening, reading, and the reproduction of what is told and read."

The solution lies in a transformation of classroom design. "There must be more actual material, more *stuff*, more appliances, and more opportunities for doing things, before the gap can be overcome" (MW 9:162). Students must be able to change the organization of their desks in order to work in small groups. In order to facilitate the continuity between ideas and cognition on the one hand, and the experiences of children on the other, school architects should take into account the need for gardens, laboratories (MW 9:169), and kitchens (LW 13:57).

Education Is an End in Itself

An education centered on occupations and carried on under such conditions would be compromised if each stage of the process were not understood as an end in itself. Each step in the process of formation has only one end, that of extracting the maximum from the students' experiences. "In our search for aims in education, we are not concerned, therefore, with finding an end outside of the educative process to which education is subordinate" (MW 9:107). As traditionally carried out, education violates this precept. It rather "exhibits a subordination of the living present to a remote and precarious future" (MW 14:185). For Dewey, education is not this sort of preparation. It is tied to growth, which in turn signifies "a constant reorganizing or reconstructing of experience."

The end of education is not to be located outside the process of educating. "It has all the time an immediate end, and so far as activity is educative, it reaches that end—the direct transformation of the quality of experience" (MW 9:82). Education is not narrowly instrumental. Dewey rejects the understanding of education that would see it as a sort of ladder to be kicked aside once a new plateau has been reached. Such a view would understand education as a mere instrument or means to attain preordained goals.

For Dewey, education is always an activity of the present. It is the practice of extracting meaning from actually existing conditions. Earlier educative experiences cannot be compared to some instrument, once used and now discarded. They are, rather, important ingredients in growth that have been absorbed as we continue life's journey. Since this is the case, each phase of that journey is to be esteemed for what it is. "Infancy, youth, adult life," according to Dewey, "all stand on the same educative level." This is so for two reasons. First, "what is really *learned* at any and every stage of experience constitutes the value of that experience." Second, "it is the chief business of life at every point to make living thus contribute to an enrichment of its own perceptible meaning" (MW 9:82).

Education as the "constant reorganizing or reconstructing of experience" is a process that is coextensive with human life itself. If education were preparation, it would have a fixed terminus at which the educative process would be finished. Such an instrumentalist attitude is reinforced by the divorce of schooling from life. But if schooling and life remain married, as Dewey suggests, then the aim of drawing from the present what is most fulfilling is a process of formation that should not stop at any stage of growth.

Education and Democracy

Whereas dualism was the great Deweyan foil, allowing him to articulate the path to be avoided, democracy provided the ideal which allowed him to identify the trail to be charted. As we saw in the last chapters, "democracy" for Dewey identifies a way of life, an ideal of social association that cannot be identified with any particular historical embodiment. As such, democracy is an ongoing experiment, open always to the possibility of amelioration.

In a Deweyan context, we should not speak of democratic societies as if they were fully in place. Rather it would be better to speak of societies attempting to become more and more democratic, struggling against the ever-present forces which tempt them away from the further realization of democratic ideals.

Summarizing themes from the previous two chapters, we can say that the level of democratization is linked to the presence of three characteristics:

1. A democratic society is one which encourages "individuality" as opposed to "individualism." Working within a biological context, Dewey accepts a "cellular" conception of societies. These are composed on the basis, not of isolated individuals, but of individuals in relation with others. The ultimate unit is not the Daltonian simple atom. The ultimate unit is an already diversified, complex cell. This cellular conception of society leads Dewey to make a distinction between individualism, the ideal of autonomy in a Lockean world, and individuality which he understands as identifying the proper manner in which each person can contribute to the community. It is this latter which needs to be cultivated.

2. Democratic societies are committed to several generative ideals, the most important of which are freedom and equality. Freedom, for Dewey, is not simply the absence of constraints. He understands it concretely as the capacity, the ability to carry out projects in practice. Equality, for him, is not identity. Equality means the recognition of the uniqueness, the irreplaceability of each human being.

    Neither freedom nor equality in its fullest manifestation is an original given. Both are emergent, growing realities. The capacities that define the extent of one's concrete freedom are but possibilities outside of association with others. Humans expand their abilities, and thus their freedom, by learning from, and working with others. The irreplaceability that is the mark of democratic equality is minimal without that development of abilities which can only be effected through social life.

3. The third element was not sufficiently emphasized in the previous chapters. A democratic way of life is being fulfilled where the different groupings that make up the society have porous boundaries. Societies become more and more democratic when there are ever more shared interests between the

differing social strata. Societies marked by rigid boundaries between social strata, even if they practice universal suffrage, are minimally democratic. Such societies remain too closely aligned to the aristocratic model.

Democratic societies are judged by the manner in which there is ample interaction and movement between social strata. Where the interaction is fluid and the movement is free, there the ideal of democracy is closest to realization. Where there are polarization, fixed distinctions, and hardly any shared interests, there the ideal of democracy is farthest from realization. A more vibrant democratic life would channel energy in a different direction. "It signifies a society in which every person shall be occupied in something which makes the lives of others better worth living, and which accordingly makes the ties which bind persons together more perceptible—which breaks down the barriers of distance between them" (MW 9:326).

Each of these three themes translates into propositions for educational reform:

1. A system of education in a democratic society must not only be open to all its citizens, but must make a concerted effort to succeed in well educating them. In practice, this means paying attention to the differing situations of children entering the educational system.[3] The supposition of absolute equality as an original given must be rejected. Otherwise, the result is a system which merely reinforces the benefits of privileged birth, together with the drawbacks of a less favorable one.

2. The educational system must help increase freedom as power to select and accomplish adequate life-projects. It must also foster the growth of individuality. The school can do this by structuring itself as a community which emphasizes shared goals and group projects.

3. Democratic education must widen the scope of student interests. Understanding history, the sciences, painting, music and literature are the prerequisites to breaking down barriers between classes and establishing a context for wider shared interests. Without education in these areas, the class distinctions which separate those who work with their hands and those who do not is magnified, not attenuated.

4. Education in a democratic society must also inculcate the
    habits of taking account of others prior to making decisions.
    The democratic way of life is not dominated by the attitudes
    summarized in the slogans "Leave me alone," "Do your own
    thing,"or "It's up to the individual." These are precisely what
    democratic life does *not* prize. Democratic practice is marked
    by taking others into account, by considerations of conse-
    quences and how they impact beyond their immediately per-
    ceived benefit for the agent.

Each social grouping, claims Dewey, will share at least one
common aim or interest. That is precisely what identifies it as a
specific grouping. Each grouping will also share, to a certain
degree, relations with other groups (MW 9:89). Large, complex
contemporary societies are composed, not of isolated individuals,
but of individuals linked to others in various ways: families,
clubs, social organizations, ethnicity, business associations. The
composite units of a nation are, as we have already seen, always
smaller societies.

This is not to say that a successful democratic society is but
a concatenation of isolated groups. To forge a national identity,
there must be developed a sense of shared ideals and goals.
There must be some degree of "like-mindedness" (MW 9:7). "A
society is a number of people held together because they are
working along common lines, in a common spirit, and with reference to common aims. The common needs and aims demand a
growing interchange of thought and growing unity of sympathetic feeling" (MW 1:10). A state which considers itself democratic is successful to the extent (1) that the various groups share
some interests in common, and (2) that there is a flexibility of
relations between them.

The danger is always that of becoming, or of reverting to a
society with fixed classes. The exemplary trajectory for democratic societies is the movement away from their aristocratic
antecedents, and toward a society where the social relations are
entirely flexible. Contemporary societies wishing to become more
fully democratic must make the effort to avoid slipping back into
various forms of aristocracy by establishing as a central goal
the continual struggle against all forms of polarization between
social classes.

One great challenge for education thus becomes that of
expanding the citizens' range of interests. Individuals whose affil-

iations rest on the basis of say, ethnicity, or shared attraction to sports, music, mountain climbing, will continue to associate with other like-minded individuals. But a nation only composed of such groupings, separated one from the others, will not have made progress beyond the fixed classifications of aristocratic societies. Democracy, as an ideal of social organization, necessitates fluidity and not fixity. Even the presence of a free press and universal suffrage, on this Deweyan view, are no guarantees of a fully flourishing democratic society. Such factors are but means which help in the construction of a democratic society.

Once this background is understood, the important role of education in a Deweyan democracy can more fully be grasped. The role of schooling is usually considered to be that of assuring the presence of an educated electorate, one well prepared to make careful choices at the polling booth. But the Deweyan landscape is more topographically complex than this. An educated electorate which would continue a politics which reinforced the separations between, and the limitations on, social groups, is an electorate which is only in the incipient stages of building a democratic society.

Education in democratic communities faces the task of enlarging the horizons of its participants, so that there are multiple opportunities for people from different social groups to share common interests. Education must attempt to foster the greatest amount of criss-crossing and zig-zagging of concerns among the populace. The greater the degree and breadth of shared interests, the closer is a society to the democratic model. The goal is "capacity to share in the give and take of experience."

> It covers all that makes one's experience more worth while to others, and all that enables one to participate more richly in the worthwhile experiences of others. Ability to produce and to enjoy art, capacity for recreation, the significant utilization of leisure, are more important elements in it than elements conventionally associated oftentimes with citizenship. (MW 9:127)

The greatest enemy to democratic practice then becomes the sharp separation of education into liberal, cultural schooling for the elite, and vocational training for the masses.

Democratic societies must move toward a "course of study which should be useful and liberal at the same time" (MW 9:267).

The good citizen, says Dewey, is "not simply the man who can vote and use his influence to get good government." To speak of a good citizen as a "useful" citizen is perfectly appropriate, so long as the word "useful" is properly understood. Within a Deweyan framework, a "useful" citizen is "one who can enjoy life and employ his leisure time in a socially profitable way." Such an individual "has capacity for appreciation of art, science, history, and literature for their own sake" (MW 15:167).

We cannot hope for immediate perfect fluidity between all the various social groups within a society. Nor should there be established the goal of a perfectly homogeneous, undifferentiated mass of individuals as populating a democratic society. Large societies will always be "cellular," composed of multiple smaller societies. What democracies can do, however, is work toward improving social fluidity. What they must most guard against is rigidity and polarization.

Moral Education

Such considerations mean that, for Dewey, all education is moral education. Whether recognized or not, the pedagogical techniques, the subject-matter selected, the choice of texts, the arrangement of the classroom, all tend to reinforce certain habits and to weaken others. The proper ordering of habits being a central concern in moral philosophy, education cannot hide behind the illusory ideal of neutrality.

Early in the history of philosophy, Aristotle pointed out the direct connection between a nation's constitution and its educational system.

> The citizen should be molded to suit the form of government under which he lives. For each government has a peculiar character which originally formed and which continues to preserve it. The character of democracy creates democracy, and the character of oligarchy creates oligarchy; and always the better the character, the better the government. (Aristotle, *Politics*, 1337a11–17)

Education does not take place in a vacuum. Each particular kind of society provides guidance as to the sort of exemplary character that ought to be encouraged. There is no such thing as a neutral education. Even an education purporting to be neutral would, in fact, be subsumed under a working ideal, that of inculcating suspension of judgment with regard to questions of good and bad. Neutrality, in other words, would be considered an important good.

Dewey's suggestions for reform in education are wholly consistent with the Aristotelian attitude. His notion of an exemplary citizen is articulated in line with his understanding of what democracy means. What has to be recognized with regard to schooling is that moral education does not take place by means of sermons and exhortations. Adding a battery of ethics courses, for example, is not the way to improve the moral education of children. To use a Deweyan distinction, this latter process would involve learning "ideas about morality" rather than "moral ideas." Moral ideas are those which "take effect in conduct and improve it, make it better than it otherwise would be" (MW 4:267).

Character is always being shaped by the experiences that the child undergoes. Democratic education must be aware of this fact and utilize it toward its own ends. The challenge faced by educators, "is to see to it that the greatest possible number of ideas acquired by children and youth are acquired in such a vital way that they become *moving* ideas, motive-forces in the guidance of conduct." Once the Asomatic Attitude is set aside, the boundary between "pure" learning and social behavior is dissolved. Ideas become "vital" and "moving." "This demand and this opportunity make the moral purpose universal and dominant in all instruction—whatever the topic" (MW 4:267).

Within a democratic context this universal moral purpose is subordinated to the social ideal. Contrary to nineteenth-century thinking, Dewey does not believe that democratic societies exist mainly to allow individuals to do as they please. The democratic ideal is a social one, it seeks to promote a way of life that provides the optimal conditions for living together. Because of this, the moral end of schooling is to develop habits that encourage working together well with others.

Interest in community welfare, an interest that is intellectual and practical, as well as emotional—an interest, that is to say, in perceiving whatever makes for social order and progress, and in carrying these principles into execution—is the moral habit to which all the special school habits must be related if they are to be animated by the breath of life. (MW 4:274)

To make such an "interest in community welfare" a guiding interest, the democratic community must seek to inculcate a combination of habits. There must be (1) habits appropriate for any
type of culture, for example, punctuality, neatness, dependability, and (2) those especially appropriate to democratic life—cooperation, flexibility, concern for the welfare of others.

In order to provide the circumstances within which such
habits can be encouraged, the most important prerequisite is
that schools themselves be thought of as communities. Children
are to be habituated from their earliest schooling into those dispositions and behaviors needed for successful participation in
community life. When the students are thus properly introduced
to a life that takes account of others, "we shall have the deepest
and best guarantee of a larger society which is worthy, lovely,
and harmonious" (MW 1:19–20).

If the school is to foster certain habits that will make an
impact on the life of the wider community, it cannot be an isolated island cut off from that community. The child cannot be
given the impression that certain sorts of behavior are appropriate in school, but that since school involves an artificial suspension of everyday life, those behaviors are merely specific to
school life. Such an attitude Dewey labels as "formal" moral
training. The encouraged duties are "distinctly school duties,
not life duties" (MW 4:274).

Once the school is recognized as a little community, pedagogical techniques must be employed which are consistent with
the moral aims of education. In a democratic society, these aims
should lead to the development of "a vital social spirit or to methods that appeal to sympathy and cooperation instead of to
absorption, exclusiveness, and competition" (MW 4:279). The
pedagogy which best suits this aim, is also the one that most recognizes the integral nature of human beings. They are not empty
minds waiting for content to be poured in. Humans are intelligent, embodied creatures. They are active, experimental, and
curious. What they need is the guidance into shared undertakings which will build on their natural impulses.

The Deweyan classroom thus unites the two concerns that
represent the foci around which this chapter is built, a view of
human nature, and an understanding of democracy. It must,
as we have already seen, treat education as an end in itself. "If at
whatever period we choose to take a person, he is still in process

of growth, then education is not, save as a by-product, a preparation for something coming later. Getting from the present the degree and kind of growth there is in it is education" (MW 12:185). Education as preparation encourages the wrong sorts of habits: those of competitiveness and individual achievement at the expense of others, traits already amply prevalent in our society. "Moreover, as a rule, it will be found that remote success is an end which appeals most to those in whom egoistic desire to get ahead—to get ahead of others—is already only too strong a motive" (MW 4:277).

The emphasis on individual competitiveness is also reinforced if the classroom does not encourage activity and the development of a child's natural curiosity. Pedagogy must always attempt to bring the children into active participation rather than mere passive absorption. The classroom built around recitation, where all students read the same passages at the same time, and all repeat what the instructor is saying, is a classroom where coordinated activity toward an end is completely absent. "There is next to no opportunity for any social division of labor. There is no opportunity for each child to work out something specifically his own, which he may contribute to the common stock, while he, in turn, participates in the productions of others" (MW 4:275).

Working together on projects can, by contrast, help bring out in a child a sense of contribution. It can help inculcate the attitude that others are not obstacles to be overcome on the way to individual success. Our co-citizens can be seen as offering opportunities for working toward a shared outcome that could not emerge but for concerted, cooperative effort. The motivation, in such a case, is intrinsic, linked to the cumulative working out of an end, not extrinsic, based on fear of a poor grade or desire to impress a teacher.

The world outside the school is one in which we need to work with others. A democratic society puts a premium on considering others prior to undertaking actions. Schooling, in a Deweyan context, is simply an activity which is continuous with these larger surroundings. It is not a refuge. Nor is it the mere servant of industry, training people for fixed professions. The school is one of the many communities which make up the national community. It is a microcosm which should (1) reflect the macrocosm, and (2) encourage the sorts of habits that will optimize the chances of a flourishing democratic life.

To summarize, education in a democratic society has multiple goals:

1. It must accentuate the value of immediate experience, considering it not only as a means to future results. This is the educational corollary to the recognition of each individual's inherent value. Education must seek to bring out the significance of the present. Contemporary experience, including that of the classroom, has intrinsic value. It does not simply serve as a means to distant goals. Education, says Dewey, is not preparation.
2. Education must widen the interests of students. This helps liberate them for multiple and diverse relations with their fellow citizens. It also allows them to develop their "individuality," the unique manner in which they can contribute to social well-being.
3. Finally, education must habituate students for community life. This life is marked most of all, by a decision-making process that is not carried out in a vacuum. Decisions are made neither by individual acts of will nor by individuals who claim insight into absolute truths. The process, rather, involves a willingness to take into account the information provided by others as well as their desires and situations.

At this point the analysis of democracy and the formulations of philosophical anthropology flow together and blend into the new reform stream for which Dewey is famous: education must be rooted in the experience of the students (LW 13:49), the teacher becomes less of a robot calling out phrases to be repeated and becomes rather a "leader of group activities" (LW 13:37), the idea of a monolithic, rigidly identical course of studies for all schools is "out of the question" (LW 13:52), schools must become microcosms of the community, not totally separate entities. "In place of a school set apart from life as a place for learning lessons, we have a miniature social group in which study and growth are incidents of present shared experience" (MW 9:368).

Each of these suggestions is consistent with the Deweyan project of moving beyond modern man:

1. Bodily activity, rather than be rejected, is integrated into the daily life of the school.

2. Mind is identified with the fully embodied growth of power to recognize meanings, and not as an empty container.

3. The inherently social nature of humans means that schools must be small communities. "Apart from participation in social life, the school has no moral end nor aim" (MW 4:271).

6

Making

Art versus arts

"Aesthetics" is a relatively new plant in the philosophical garden. Its origins can be specified with regard to time, the eighteenth century, and place, Germany.[1] "Reason" and "Truth" were the twin gods of the epoch. Kant and Newton were its giants. Revealed religion and speculative metaphysics were in full retreat before the dual assault of critical philosophy and scientific method. In the midst of this intellectual ferment, a new sprout saw the light of day, Art with an uppercase "A."

Neither pre-Modern Europe nor non-European cultures had felt any need for this entity. Such cultures engaged in a multiplicity of arts. There was no Galilean Purification resulting in a sharp distinction between craft and fine art.[2] The arts were integrated into the everyday life of a community. They could be useful in the service of religion or pedagogy, and they were often entertaining.

In opposition to this, as R. G. Collingwood has pointed out, the eighteenth century had established a sharp demarcation between "fine" and "useful" arts. The "fine" arts meant "not delicate or highly skilled arts, but 'beautiful' arts (*les beaux arts, le belle arti, die schöne Kunst*)" (Collingwood, 6). Kant had grappled with the difficult problems of making sense of and room for the arts so conceived within the rigid world of Enlightenment rationality. Those who followed him faced the same difficult task, but resorted to different, often conflicting ways for dealing with it.

Some philosophers, mostly German, sought to establish Art as a rival to Reason in the determination of truth. Schopenhauer, for example, echoing Plato's *Ion*, celebrated artistic creation as the "work of genius whose effect . . . is far removed from all reflection and conscious intention, and might be called an inspiration." The composer of music "reveals the inner nature of the world, and expresses the profoundest wisdom in a language that his reasoning faculty does not understand" (Schopenhauer, 260). Hegel had already established this trend by claiming that it was in works of Art that we would find "an unfolding truth that is not limited to the sphere of merely natural evolution but reveals itself in world-history" (Paolucci, 200).[3]

At the other end of the spectrum, positivists were dismissing Art as simply an outlet for the discharge of emotions. They celebrated science as the prophet of the era's twin gods, "Reason" and "Truth." Science, as Reason incarnate, provided the only access to Truth. The Schopenhauers and Hegels of the world were misguided idolaters. They worshipped the false prophet "Art," foolishly believing it would lead them to Truth. Discourse about works of art, aesthetic criticism, as A. J. Ayer asserted, aims "not so much to give knowledge as to communicate emotion" (Ayer, 113).

Others, wishing to preserve a privileged place for "Art," while also rejecting the Schopenhauer-type linkage of Art with Truth, succumbed to the Plotinian Temptation. They sought to identify what exactly was *the* trait that separated Art from all other human productions. Clive Bell's famous book *Art* was influential in this respect. In it, the essentialist drive to identify a single distinguishing characteristic is articulated with breathtaking clarity. The pre-Modern maelstrom which failed to separate Art from craft was muddled and needed to be overcome. Bell claimed that "all sensitive people" (i.e., all like-minded British intellectuals) "agree that there is a peculiar emotion provoked by works of art" (Bell, 6). The property which gives rise to this emotion is "significant form." In all genuine works of Art "lines and colors combined in a particular way, certain forms and relations of forms, stir our aesthetic emotions" (Bell, 8). Bell thus articulated an understanding of art well suited to the nonrepresentational revolution in the visual arts at the turn of the century in Europe.

Finally, there is the asomatic version of aestheticism embodied in Oscar Wilde's *The Picture of Dorian Gray*. "Art" continued to be understood as inhabiting a province separate from the everyday occurrences of life. Indeed, its main role was identified as providing solace and refuge from the trials, difficulties, and shortcomings of ordinary life. The novel is constructed along an axis which opposes higher and lower, purity and contamination. Art is the home of the pure, elevated, and detached aspirations of human life. In Art we can find an escape from the bodily rhythms of time (childhood, adolescence, maturity, age) and the social rhythms of community life (mutual obligation, responsibility, consequences of mistaken choices). Art is what refreshes and cleanses. Dorian goes to the opera to forget his role in Sibyl Vane's suicide. "And besides, my dear old Basil, if you really want to console me, teach me rather to forget what has happened, or to see it from the proper artistic point of view. Was it not Gautier who used to write about *la consolation des arts*?" (Wilde, 140). Art must be pure and elevated if humans are to escape, be it only briefly, from the pull and weight of being caught in a material world.

Each of these ways of understanding art is built on a specifically Modern European assumption: replacing arts with Art. The generous pre-Modern embrace of the arts as both encompassing what today we would call "crafts," and as integrated within community life, was set aside. In its place the eighteenth and nineteenth centuries celebrated "Art." Prior to that time, (and since that time), humans have been engaged in making many sorts of things: buildings, linens, gardens, pottery, masks, music, sculpture, theatre, poetry. There were many arts, but no "Art."

The new arena of reflection, "aesthetics," did not simply discover what had heretofore remained unrecognized. It cut out, highlighted, and isolated as a separate component of reality, what was previously woven into the fabric of cultural existence. In so doing, it elevated to a new plane the maker of Art. "In the later nineteenth century the artist walked among us as a superior being, marked off even by his dress from common mortals" (Collingwood, 5). The word "artist" was no longer appropriate for those involved in multifarious modes of fabricating works out of various materials. Some special ones among them were now thought to be "creators" in the service of a rarified ideal called "Art."

For some time this invention was championed as positive and progressive. Then, in the twentieth century, there came signs of a reassessment. André Malraux, for one, conceded the fairly recent birth of "Art." "Neither the ancient East, nor the Middle Ages, had conceived of the idea we express in the word 'art'" (Malraux, 207).[4] Contemporary collectors and curators search out and identify "masterpieces" of the past. But these "were created by artists for whom the idea of art did not exist"

(Malraux, 210). "A Romanesque crucifix was not regarded by its contemporaries as a work of sculpture; nor Cimabue's *Madonna* as a picture, even Pheidias' *Pallas Athene* was not, primarily, a statue" (Malraux, 9).[5]

For the new hybrid aesthetics/Art to thrive, the soil in which it was planted had to be suitably prepared. Aesthetic theory found this fertile ground in the dualistic biases of modernity: disjunction of mind from body, reason from emotion, and the subject/object bifurcation. The new growth also required great care. It did not flourish naturally. Some sort of greenhouse was needed to keep it alive. This accommodation was provided by another invention of modernity, the museum. Museums "imposed on the spectator a wholly new attitude toward the work of art. They have tended to estrange the works they bring together from their original functions and to transform even the portraits into 'pictures'" (Malraux, 9).

Malraux foresaw a new world populated by "museums without walls." The perfecting of photography meant that reproductions could be examined by a large number of individuals. It also meant that works not suitable for museums, site-specific statues, frescoes, statuary from Asia and Africa, could now be given a far more expanded exposure (Malraux, 12). Still, for Malraux, the museum without walls did not challenge the notion of "Art." It simply widened its availability.

By contrast, a fundamental challenge to "Art" is exactly the task undertaken by Dewey. He critiques the very notion of a museum conception of art (LW 10:14). Museums reinforce the belief that works of art are something separate from the milieu of ordinary life. The developments of capitalism, nationalism, and imperialism have been powerful vectors in constituting art "objects" as possessions whose value can be calculated in monetary terms, in terms of national pride, or of cultural and military superiority. The narrow, essentialist assumptions that only certain "inspired" individuals in certain "fine" arts deserve the title "artist," and that their productions are to be kept separate from ordinary life, are now put into question.

Dewey admits that prior philosophy has transformed art works into "specimens of fine art and nothing else" (LW 10:15). But for him such a transformation is not to be celebrated. Indeed, it helps identify the problem: "that of recovering the continuity of aesthetic experience with normal processes of living" (LW 10:16). Asking for such a recovery undermines the separations of Art from life and reason from emotion that underlie the various interpretations of art mentioned at the beginning of this chapter. Recovering "the continuity of aesthetic experience with normal processes of living" is no easy task. It is obstructed by the double hierarchy growing out of nineteenth-century aesthetics.[6] The Plotinian Temptation toward unity is here undertaken in a two-step fashion. First of all, several arts were privileged as encompassing "fine" Art (typically, architecture, sculpture, painting, poetry, and music). The hierarchization was then crowned by the selection of one among these as *the* fullest manifestation of Art. For Schopenhauer this was music. For Hegel and Heidegger, it was poetry. Kandinsky, not surprisingly, identified painting as that art which can best lead one away from matter and into the realm of the spiritual.[7]

This hierarchization is flatly rejected by Dewey. The restrictive notion that "paintings, statues, poems, songs and symphonies" represent "fineness" in Art is "conventional." What is "fine" does not depend upon membership in a preselected, privileged caste. Fineness is not based upon antecedent categories, but on accomplishment. Whenever a work of human fabrication provides both an immediate sense of satisfaction, and occasions our desire to seek out what is refined, that work is worthy of the label "fine." "Any activity that is productive of objects whose perception is an immediate good, and whose operation is a continual source of enjoyable perception of other events exhibits fineness of art" (LW 1:274).

"Making" is an ongoing process that includes both what the artist fabricates, and what the art work itself prompts as it enters into community experience. Dewey turns away from the artificial cultivation of a wholly independent category "Art." The makings associated with what came to be called the "fine arts" do not exhaust human creativity. Once the biases of the eighteenth and nineteenth centuries have been overcome, marginalized arts such as garden and park design can be welcomed into the fold. But that is not all. Artisans and engineers, long forgotten relatives, are reinstated as members of the artistic family. Pottery, quilting, and dance, as well as bridge building and subway design can all exhibit fineness. What counts is not an antecedent commitment to a specialized notion of "Art." What counts instead is the way in which an activity is carried out. A Danish woman weaving a Sunday apron can exhibit fineness in her art every bit as much as can Frank Stella and Christo in theirs.

Instead of Kandinsky's asomatic emphasis on the "spiritual" separated from the material, we ought rather to make good pragmatist room for the "human," a category too often either ignored or narrowly construed by the philosophical tradition. Emphasizing the human helps us grasp how "making" and its products "idealize qualities found in common experience" (LW 10:17). In so doing, we can alter the attitudes and valuations that have been dominant in Western thought since the 1700s. As Collingwood pointed out in the citation at the beginning of the chapter, the eighteenth century narrowed the extent of the arts by equating "fine" art with the "beautiful" arts. In so doing it relegated to the margins other areas of human production, even if they proved to be "delicate or highly skilled." Dewey reverses this, privileging once again the wider traits "delicate" and "highly skilled" wherever these might occur.

This chapter will attempt to outline the main themes associated with this new Deweyan understanding. Several topics are of special importance. The first has already been addressed, the very meaning of "art" itself. The second involves a central player in the philosophical vocabulary since the empiricists, "experience." The others, "imagination," "expression," and "communication," are given novel and special roles in the Deweyan analysis of art.

Experience

"Experience" is a central term in the Deweyan vocabulary. Indeed, it figures prominently in the titles Dewey chose for two of his most important works, *Experience and Nature*, and *Art as Experience*. As we saw in chapter 2, it can also be a misleading term whose eighteenth-century empiricist connotations Dewey tried, with little success, to overcome.

As he neared the end of his life, having tired of the semantic battles and explanations involving the term, he proposed to alter the title of his Carus Lectures from *Experience and Nature* to *Culture and Nature* (LW 1:361). The term "culture" he thought, so long as it was understood in the anthropological sense designating "the vast range of things experienced in an indefinite variety of ways," might be a more suitable term. There is no guarantee, however, that the word "culture," with its own cluster of meanings, would have fared any better than "experience" (LW 1:361–64).

FIGURE 6.1

John Dewey, Maple Lodge, 1949

Courtesy of John Dewey Papers, Special Collections/Morris Library, Southern Illinois University at Carbondale.

Central to his understanding of experience was the rejection of any connotation associated with mere noetic receptivity of neutral data. Experiencing is a fully human activity. It can be separated neither from human interests, nor from active experimentation. Dewey might have had less difficulty explaining his usage had his audience understood French. There, "experiment" and "experience" have roughly the reverse meanings of the English words. To say that someone is "experimented," "*elle est expérimentée*," means "she is experienced." To say of people that they are making "experiences," "*faire des expériences*," means engaging in experiments. The experiment-experience connection is crucial for understanding what Dewey means.

Contemporary English usage has made of "experience" a term dominated by connotations of passive receptivity, just the opposite of its French meaning. To revive the Deweyan sense, the word needs to be understood as an adjective. We can say of someone that she is an "experienced" pilot or an "experienced" counselor. What is meant is that the individual, via practice and involvement, together with study and reflection, has developed the habits appropriate to the successful carrying out of her functions.

Above all, "experience" is not to be understood in the empiricist sense of simply receiving impressions. This might be appropriate for a "subject" face to face with an "object," as if the mind were like film in a camera. But we are not detached spectators at the theatre. We are active, multidimensional participants in our milieu. This active participation, together with its outcomes are what Dewey terms "experience." Experimentation, reflection, and awareness of consequences are its watchwords. Experiencing is the human mode of being in the world. It designates "in a summary fashion, the complex of all which is distinctively human" (LW 1:331).

The materials of our everyday surroundings need to be woven together so that they do not merely accumulate, but rather culminate in a set of habits that provide meaningful ways of interacting with those surroundings. Someone who is experienced no longer confronts a fluid concatenation of data. There are now "meanings," events situated in an interpretive matrix. The contingent and multiple occurrences that befall an experienced pilot or a counselor are not befuddling surds. These events can now be situated within a wider context and understood accordingly. They are no longer isolated incomprehensibles. They become meaningful, that is to say, integrated elements in an overarching whole.

The process of becoming experienced, that of marshalling materials in a way that they do not merely accumulate, but culminate in some determinate, meaningful, form, is also the process that characterizes "art" for Dewey. Those whom we recognize as exemplary artists are able to carry out such activities in a heightened, refined way. "Aesthetic experience," Dewey went so far as to claim, "is experience in its integrity" (LW 10:278).

The emphasis on activity and process was occluded in traditional philosophy of art because of empiricism's bias toward mind as passive receptor of data. Armed with his richer grasp of experience, Dewey wishes to stress the entire process which begins with the artist's crafting of a work, and continues through the life of this work. By highlighting such a temporal sequence, Dewey hoped to "recover the continuity of aesthetic experience with the normal processes of living," and to learn how works of art "idealize qualities found in common experience" (LW 10:16–17).

The more common view of Art, the one which begins with finished products, can result in an outlook which opposes life to Art, as in the case of Dorian Gray. Dewey, revitalizing a pre-Modern notion, chooses instead to inscribe artistic activity within the contexts of experiencing, of living, fully human lives. This context, quite naturally, encompasses the varied makings that help us in terms of comfort, beauty, and enjoyment, and in making sense of our lives. There is no single force "Art" which has a single goal: making pure art objects suitable for disinterested contemplation. There are many types of fabricating which "idealize qualities found in common experience" while maintaining continuity with the "normal processes of living."

We are creatures who seek the good in a world that supplies no ready-made answers. That quest can best be satisfied if we make a fully human effort, combining experimentation, reflection, discussion, awareness of consequences, emotional commitment, tentative resolutions, and imaginative projection of results. In short, the fully human mode of approaching the good is neither cold rationality nor raw impulse. It is rather, experiment-experience.

Dewey's title *Art as Experience* signals his belief that making, art, is not divorced from the context of ordinary life. Indeed, it is to be understood as a refinement of what occurs naturally.

Too often, experience-experiment goes on haphazardly and incoherently in our lives. Those whom we recognize as great artists, a Frank Lloyd Wright, a Marian Anderson, a Cezanne, a Pisano, a Tschaikovsky, an Olmsted, serve as exemplars, those for whom experience culminates in productions of such refinement that they have an impact on the experiences of the community to which they belong. These products are meaningful. That is to say, they serve as means, as mediators, in subsequent experience. A Pisano pulpit, for example, not only helps give flesh and meaning to religious beliefs, but it stands also as an exemplar of how form, function, and beauty can exist in easy harmony.

Imagination, Communication, and Expression

Dewey's emphasis on the life-world and on continuity must not be interpreted in a reductionistic manner. Modernity, renewing a prominent Hellenistic theme, had, it is true, assumed a culture/nature partition. Assuming such a partition led, in turn, to a quest for recovering unalloyed nature. To succeed in this quest, "culture," viewed as an artificial accretion, had to be pared away. Rousseau's fascination with the "noble savage" and Tolstoy's fascination with peasants are two Modern manifestations of this quest.

Diogenes the Cynic (fl. 340 B.C.) had actually tried to live out the opposition between culture and nature. Rejecting all that he believed to be artificial, he wandered about carrying in a sack only a few articles of clothing and a ladle for water. Observing a child drink water with his hands, he recognized how extraneous was the ladle and jettisoned it. In a similar way, after seeing a child who had broken his plate scoop up cooked beans with some bread, Diogenes discarded his bowl (Laertius, 39). Art has little place in such a world. It is always art-ificial.

The other side of the culture/nature partition gives rise to a "spiritualized" view of art. Art's emergence from the non-natural, that is to say, the "cultural" dimension of human existence, is here embraced and celebrated. Dorian Gray is the contradictory blossom that emerged from the same seed as Diogenes. One rejects the cultural in the name of the "natural." The other escapes the natural by entering the rarified "cultural" world. Both accept the culture/nature partition that defined Modern thought. Both see art as discontinuous with the processes of everyday living. One rejects art as artificial. The other sees Art as the work of a special faculty called "imagination." The two positions are symbionts joined together by a belief in asomatism writ large, the separation of culture from nature.

The everyday world of twentieth-century life, when taken seriously as the starting point for philosophical reflection, suggests instead Deweyan continuity. Our lives are surrounded by entities that cannot be divided neatly into either cultural or natural products. Vaccines, nuclear power plants, x-rays, even Heideggerian windmills offer examples of what Bruno Latour calls "hybrids," products that take on life as the result of nature-culture cooperation (Latour, 73). Dewey's ontology of interactions would go even further and identify all products of human intellection as "hybrids," the results of organism-environment interaction.

The facile "human versus nature" bifurcation of earlier epochs had already been undermined by the post-Darwinian context within which Dewey lived. It was this context which led him to stress "continuity" as a way of avoiding both the nature/culture partition and the two forms of reductionism/escape that could result. Continuity offers a middle path. Humans are not to be confused with other animals. What distinguishes humans is the possibility of saturating life with "conscious meanings derived from communication and deliberate expression" (LW 10:28).

This triad—meanings, communication, and expression—plays an important role in Dewey's analysis of art. Each of the three prongs highlights a significant dimension of artistic activity. The derivation of meanings identifies the place of imagination. Expression is Dewey's name for the meanings that resonate from art works. Communication is what art facilitates.

Imagination

Thinkers who propose a dualistic or otherwise anticontinuity analysis of existence can view imagination as a source of the fanciful and the fantastic. When it is not situated within the framework of the biosociocultural continuity, imagination has few explanations save as an autonomous, freely creative faculty. Such a contextless imagination is the source of the utopias and fantasics which have falsely seduced humans. By situating imagination within the life-world as mediated by experience, Dewey provides an alternative context for understanding it. Within this context, imagination is considered to be a capacity for the "welding together of all elements, no matter how diverse in ordinary experience, into a new and completely unified experience" (LW 10:272).

Human beings are not telescopes, microscopes, or mirrors. They are not neutral instruments for gathering information. Interest plays a central role in what is attended to, and data come already saturated with meanings. The events in which we participate do not present themselves as a buzzing, blooming confusion. They come funded with inherited sociocultural meanings which allow us to situate them within an ordered whole. These meanings tend to become standardized to such a degree that they seem "natural," the only ones possible.

But reality, as we have already seen in chapter 1, is always richer and fuller than any single network of meanings can be. This intersection between sedimented meanings and underemphasized or undisclosed possibilities is the site where imagination plays its role. Humans need not remain within the influence of preordained interpretive grids. They can elicit those possibilities not highlighted by any particular cluster of meanings to which we have become accustomed. We do not merely mirror the existing world. We are actors engaged in the ongoing project of seeking good. Doing this requires a special sensitivity to the opportunities inherent in, but unrealized by, our milieu. "Imagination" is the term used by Dewey to identify the human capacity for discerning such opportunities.

Imagination becomes quite simply the capability to envision alternatives to present conditions. It works neither *ex nihilo* nor *ab initio*. In the world of modernity, imagination could be thought of primarily as an autonomous faculty weaving whatever fanciful worlds it could envision. This led, in turn, to a fascination with fresh starts, with erasing the past, and moving in entirely new directions. In Art, creativity came to be associated with breaking wholly new ground, inaugurating an entirely new style, rupturing radically with one's progenitors. Genuine creativity could best be established by a complete abandonment of the past.

Not surprisingly one of modernity's dominating metaphors was that of the *tabula rasa*. Some thinkers, stressing passivity, saw each new generation of humans as blank slates receiving impressions. Others, stressing activity and reform, sought to make a blank slate of the past as in the French and Bolshevik revolutions. Freud may have fastened onto one of the great unspoken myths guiding modernity when he discussed the Oedipus complex. But in a pragmatist world, sons are under no compulsion to kill their fathers in order to establish themselves. Change is always important. At its most fruitful, however, it is guided by an embodied imagination, firmly rooted in the social matrix within which it exercises its powers.

Neither the *tabula rasa* nor the Oedipus Complex have any significance in Dewey's formulations. For him, a more appropriate image is that of a garden inherited from the past. Constant effort is needed in order to sustain it by making the innovations necessary to serve the ever-altering needs of the present. Success in such a task requires that actual conditions and limitations be recognized. There need be no desire for the sort of fresh start which would make of the past a *tabula rasa*. Instead, there is an effort to change present conditions in light of some good, a better future. There is a desire to manipulate conditions so that they issue into fruitful culminations.

This requires an exploration of as yet untapped possibilities. Such an exploration is the work of imagination. Utopian fantasies proliferate if imagination is considered within modernity's bifurcated understanding of human nature. Only then can it be treated as an autonomous, nonmaterial faculty projecting ideals disconnected from the human condition. Such dualistic tendencies are strenuously avoided by Dewey. His embodied imagination works more prosaically. It takes us beyond sedimented meanings while not leaving human nature behind.

Imagination, thus interpreted, is an important ingredient in all the arts of living. The human quest of seeking the good will succeed if we examine existing conditions for unrealized possibilities. The "texture of the actual," to use a Deweyan phrase (LW 10:348), is woven from many fibers which we imbue with various dyes. Imagination helps us identify new combinations of fibers so we can arrange and then dye them in novel ways. Artistic production serves as a model of imagination at work. The architect, the musician, and the dancer explore untapped possibilities in the uses of space, sound, and movement. Those individuals whom we identify as artists engage in the sorts of activities which should be of concern to all humans. Their special status derives from the ability to do so in a refined, heightened way. The difference is not one of kind. It is one of degree, sort of like that between a Little Leaguer and a professional athlete.

Expression

When imagination is wed to makings the results are
"expressive." This is so whether the things made are buildings,
paintings, furniture, parks, quilts, symphonies, or poems.
Dewey's terminology here can be quite misleading. He is not to be
confused with those who claim that art is "self-expression" (LW
10:15). Too often the model for art as expression includes the following elements: (1) a complete idea or emotion which exists
within the artist, (2) selection of materials, and (3) a finished
product that "expresses" the complete idea or emotion. Tolstoy
provided a classic formulation of art as expression. "Art begins
when one person with the object of joining another or others to
himself in one and the same feeling, expresses that feeling by certain external indications" (Tolstoy, 121–22). On such a view, the
art product is a mere external manifestation of an internal state.

The process of interpreting such a product becomes one of
reversing the direction and going from product to the idea or
feeling possessed by the artist. For Dewey, as we have seen,
such neat inner-outer divisions do not adequately describe the
human situation. The whole point of making dialogue the paradigm of philosophical discourse is that words are not simply
external sounds for fixed, preexisting ideas. Ideas are as much
subsequent to speech as antecedent to it. They emerge within the
process of dialogue itself.

An analogous claim can be made of artistic production.
Rather than claim that any material embodiment is simply a
public "expression" of a private feeling, or that any material
embodiment will necessarily fall short of its original "spiritual"
inspiration, a Deweyan alternative would be to say that the finished product is always *more* than its original inspiration. The
effort at crafting new entities out of material components, the difficulties to be overcome, the inspiration and innovations that
come from the very working with materials, all occasion novel
modifications that become incorporated into the final product.

Such considerations lead Dewey, when he discusses expression, to avoid speaking of what an artist sought by his or her
"expression." In an area where the Plotinian Temptation to unity
has been particularly strong, Dewey has managed to resist it. The
arts are so varied, and artists so different that any reduction to
one aim, even so commonly cited a one as expression, would be
futile. Dewey thus uses the noun rarely, preferring instead to

say "objects of art are expressive" (LW 10:110). What a work of art does is to "concentrate and enlargen an immediate experience" (LW 10:277). Art, because "it expresses . . . enables us to share vividly and deeply in meanings" to which we had previously been dumb (LW 10:248).

The connection of art, expression, and meaning cannot be understood unless we recognize the importance of the product's place in the life-world. There it becomes a locus of meanings, or to say the same thing, a mediating force, a means by which we can continue the ongoing quest for self-understanding and for good. An art product is expressive because it resonates with meanings when it finds a niche in a cultural milieu. It is not, as Tolstoy would have it, the mere external garb for an internal feeling.

To highlight the difference between his emphasis on the arts as "expressive" and the view that an object is an "expression" of something already possessed by the artist, Dewey makes a distinction between an art "product" and an art "work." Art "products" encompass whatever is produced, a Japanese garden, a Wright house, Swan Lake, a Rose window, an Olmsted park. As "products" they can be considered in abstraction from their role as new mediating entities in our cultural milieu. They can be contemplated from a merely aesthetic standpoint.

Art "works," by contrast, are marked by their continued vibrancy as they live on in the interpretive and meaningful life of the community. A work of art, says Dewey, is what it does, not what it is (LW 10:9). An art "product" is potentially an art "work." It becomes a work when it is an active component in the ongoing communal quest for meaning. Such vibrancy emerges within an interpretive community, that is to say, a community engaged in a common effort to identify and secure what constitutes a good life. A painting locked away in some collector's temperature-controlled vault is the paradigmatic instance of an art "product." It is a mere object, abstracted, isolated from its appropriate cultural milieu. Such an object is not expressive. More accurately, it is only potentially expressive. Its isolation prevents it from resonating with meanings, from mediating our quest for goodness.

For an alternative more in line with Dewey's position, we can turn to a country much admired by him, China. The written character commonly rendered as "art," Tu Wei-ming tells us, "signifies the activity of planting, of cultivating fields." This root "later gave rise to its meaning of acquired skills." Ultimately, an "artist" is a "person capable of performing unusual tasks" (Tu, 60). Absent from this description are the foci associated with European modernity: contemplation, detachment, and vision. Not surprisingly, painting, the art on which so much Western aesthetic theory depends, is not even included in the six arts of classical Confucian thought: ritual, music, archery, charioteering, calligraphy, and arithmetic (Tu, 72n23).

Such a list, so strange to Western aesthetics, is not at all foreign to Dewey's understanding of art. Indeed, ritual could be used as an example of what Dewey means by art's "work." Tu describes "ritual," we might say "manners," as a discipline of the body which is "intended to transform the body into a fitting expression of the self in our ordinary daily existence." Ritual ultimately "trains us to perform routine functions in society as fully participating members" (Tu, 61). Ritual is at once an activity, a product, and a work. Its work is that of mediating our relations to others. It is not an object to be contemplated, but an experience to be lived and refined.

Closer to home, we could say that houses designed with large front porches or those designed with rear decks not only organize space differently, but work to encourage some sorts of interactions and minimize the importance of others. A novel like Ralph Ellison's *Invisible Man* continues to be a work as it shapes our understanding of African Americans and occasions reflections about racial issues in our country. Sometimes, artistic productions such as the paintings of the Hudson Valley school cease to do much work and become more and more mere products. At other times the process is reversed, and what had become "products" take on a renewed vibrancy as they reenter the community of interpretation. The paintings of Berthe Morisot, for example, have become once again a locus for discourse as the women's movement occasions renewed attention to female painters.

It is in this sense that art works are "expressive" for Dewey. They can provide the sort of mediation which is both a liberation and a release, a recognition of "what actual existence actually becomes when its possibilities are fully expressed" (LW 10:285). What is thus expressed is not a subjective feeling. It is rather a sense of culmination felt because forces and materials have been brought together into a meaningful whole. A harmonious conjunction is expressed out of multiple possibilities. Art works are like little life-worlds. They are richer, more complex and multifaceted than any of our attempts to give them a fixed meaning.

To indicate the inexhaustible trove of meanings manifested by works of art at their best, Dewey chose the word "expressive."

This conjunction, in turn, continues to be expressed as it works to shape our desires, interactions, and comprehensions of the world. As Tu puts it, the six arts transform us from people who have merely the "buds" or "sprouts" of human possibility into centers of fruitful relationships. "As a center, a person never loses his proper location whenever and wherever he happens to be: the profound person always feels at home" (Tu, 62). Profound persons feel at home because the milieu of existence, mediated by their arts, now expresses a cosmos, an ordered whole. The road, as Cervantes noted, is better than the inn. Better still, Dewey and Tu might add, is the home.

Dewey is not, however, a naive optimist. He realizes that this working of art in the community is not always successful. It may be hampered by many factors. Its greatest enemy is routine. A fully routinized life is one surrounded by "products." It is one for which the rich meanings of objects and events have been reduced to conventionalized redundancies. Such a life circulates within a rigid preordained grid imposed on the possibilities of existence. Arthur Miller's troubled salesman, Willy Loman, is caught in such a grid. Life is thought to involve fixed goals, the context is assumed to be unchanging, and existence provides stimuli to which one responds in preprogrammed ways for attaining the fixed goals. Willy Loman and Dorian Gray exist at opposite ends of the spectrum. Dorian lives above the push and pull of everyday existence. Willy's life is a caricature of someone who has for too long believed in a faulty cluster of myths. He is completely imbedded in a life whose self-interpretation is limited and limiting. Because he cannot liberate himself from the strictures of the interpretive grid, Willy is beaten when it is no longer adequate to changing conditions. There is no liberation for Willy because sedimentation has blinded him to the mediating factors that might allow recognition of alternatives. Dorian Gray, on the other hand, believes that liberation means escape not only from the humdrum of ordinary existence, but also from its gnawing, inconvenient moral sentiments.

Dewey seeks a middle road between these two extremes. The expressiveness of art as experience is liberating, but it is not an escape. The liberation comes from an art work's manifesting possibilities newly realized. A grandmother's quilt, recently acquired, may, for example, express a combination of love, skill, beauty, and utility that is too often lacking in the contemporary world. An art work is a novel existence which first of all expresses its own combination of possibilities. In addition, its mediating potential continues so long as it forms part of the life-world. The interpretive frameworks to which it gives rise are as diverse as are the peoples and times whose cultures it touches. Art works liberate by immersing us in a fuller, wider world, not by removing us from that world.

This immersion, at its best, is a social phenomenon. The quality of a culture, Dewey maintains, is determined by "the arts which flourish" (LW 10:347). The task of achieving a good life can be realized by bringing to life the ideals that are latent in surrounding conditions. The makings of artists serve as constant reminders that such realizations are possible. "Art is the living and concrete proof that man is capable of restoring consciously, and thus on the plane of meaning, the union of sense, need, impulse and action characteristic of the live creature" (LW 10:31). Art is "experience," the "union of sense, need, impulse and action" carried to its culmination.

Art as experience, as an ongoing work, minimizes the chances that we will understand ourselves as spectators. Within the Deweyan synthesis, painting is displaced as the premier art. That it took on this role can be understood given the network of assumptions guiding modernity. Clive Bell, heir to these assumptions, could even write a book entitled *Art* and concern himself with "visual art" (Bell, 7). The Deweyan position would encourage us to be, not spectators, but participants. Our experiment-experiences should involve the attempts to incorporate the materials of life and fashion them as manifestations of imaginatively projected ideals. Since human life is social, such a constant search for the ideals-to-be-realized requires a common effort. The condition for that common effort, a process that harmonizes, is what Dewey refers to as communication.

Communication

Democratic life is that form of social organization which, as we have seen, aims at flexible boundaries between social groups. Societies are democratic in proportion to the amount and variety of interactions that take place between the diverse elements that make up the public. The best of these interactions involve shared participation in common activities. This shared participation is what Dewey calls "communication."

Societies move away from the democratic ideal when they are fragmented, rigidly layered, or compartmentalized. In those cases the interactions between the groups which make them up are "external and mechanical" (LW 10:337). These are noncommunicating interactions. They are "only to a slight degree forms of communicative intercourse" (LW 10:338). As we enter the twenty-first century, American society appears to be more and more filled with "non-communicating interactions," including, in some cases, those between artists and communities whose lives are touched by their creations.[8]

To this degree, contemporary American society is far from the democratic ideal as envisioned by Dewey. A democratic community is marked by a high degree of "communication." There must be ample zig-zagging and criss-crossing of interests that weave a harmonious whole out of diverse elements. Such zig-zagging and criss-crossing need to take place within a social field whose boundaries and playing rules are generally agreed upon. Art can be instrumental in preparing such a social field. Physical life, says Dewey, cannot live without a physical environment, and "moral life cannot exist without a moral environment." "Desire and purpose" are affected even by the "technological arts" (LW 10:347). What surrounds us also directs us. In other words, what surrounds us expresses a cluster of possibilities, encourages a certain combination of interactions, and helps to shape our desires.

Life is always a matter of choices. Choices depend on attention. But we cannot take in all of our milieu. Attention is of necessity selective. What we emphasize, highlight, and show concern for, is not predetermined from birth. Interest and attention are, to a great degree, culturally conditioned. Because the arts determine what surround us (the design of our cities and buildings, our sites for recreation, the stories which hold our attention, the music to which we listen, the memorials, sculptures and paintings which populate our public and private spaces), they are a dominant factor in educating our desires. As such, they help determine the shared undertakings considered important in a community.

Distraction versus Participation

Once we move beyond the conception of "Art" that has been dominant for three centuries, we come to realize how art works are not just the prized, expensive commodities displayed in museums. Art works are not elsewhere, they are all around us. Optimistic as he was, Dewey did not spend enough time discussing the ways these works might be bad, distasteful, and ugly. They can occasion participation in narrow, self-interested, disintegrative activities, just as well as they can be means to a richer, more ample fulfillment of our lives.

This is an important realization, not developed adequately by Dewey, that we nonetheless must confront if we are to follow him. Because we are constantly bathed in an environment conditioned by art works, they are most important with regard to creating a milieu which encourages certain aspirations while discouraging others. Occasioning a world in which the social field will be fruitful is a challenge faced by all communities. Its very undertaking is compromised, however, so long as the arts are confused with Art. "As long as art is the beauty parlor of civilization," says Dewey, "neither art nor civilization is secure" (LW 10:346).

When the arts forming our lifeworld are vibrant, positive forces in society, we are inclined to follow their process of organizing material in light of certain ideals. When the arts are merely mechanical, they occasion, by contrast a response which itself is mechanical. Human life is then reduced to the stimulus-response model. This is why Dewey identifies "routine" as the great foil of art as experience.

Unfortunately the arts of pop culture, those which affect the largest numbers of people, can tend toward this direction. They present us, as Thomas Alexander aptly puts it, with "the same disguised as the different" (Alexander, 1987b, 6). The role they play is mostly that of offering "relief from the project of life" (Alexander 1987b, 5). They do not so much "work" to draw us into participation, as amuse while encouraging passivity.

Music videos, romance novels, soap operas encourage us to assume that we are completed selves. As such, our desires are thought to be fixed. Interactions then become primarily ways of considering others as possible means for the satisfaction of those desires. Experience-experiment, as encompassing the fully human way of living, is thereby minimized. Popular culture can thus work to reinforce the status quo. It can transform the lifeworld into a narrow grid of stimuli to which we respond in predetermined ways.

This awareness of how far some popular arts are from the Deweyan ideal of genuine expressiveness might lead us, erroneously, to make a sharp division between elite and popular art. This would be a mistake because, for Dewey, the only distinction worth making is that between "fine" and not so fine arts, not that between high and popular art. Fineness is the key to fine arts, and fineness is not necessarily opposed to popularity. Routine, redundancy, escapism are the enemies of fineness. The popularity of an art work, in itself, is an irrelevant factor.[9]

Albert Murray's writings on African American music, for example, though seemingly composed without any knowledge of Deweyan aesthetics, give voice to a Deweyan-type position. The "artless," Murray points out, is characterized by conformity, predictability, the "same old stuff time and again" (Murray, 1976, 207–8). Such artlessness cannot do justice to the complexities of black experience in contemporary America. Those artists who have done justice to these complexities were both popular and refined.

> Louis Armstrong knew better than that and so did Jelly Roll Morton, King Oliver, and Duke Ellington—as did Charlie Parker, Dizzy Gillespie, Miles Davis and Thelonius Monk, all of whom extended, elaborated and refined that folk stuff as far as talent and craft enabled them. (Murray, 1996, 4)

Murray speaks of Duke Ellington as a "playful improviser." Such playfulness followed by dedicated musicians culminates in that "measure of elegance" that takes a work to "that special level of stylization known as fine art" (Murray, 1996, 107).

Such playful options are essential to art as experience. Without them, we tend to regard ourselves as completed selves. For completed selves, routine, redundancy, predictability are the rule. Lived experience, by contrast, should help us become aware of how we are not completed selves. The centrality of improvisation in blues and jazz is expressive of just this point. So are the metaphors used by Tu Wei-Ming in his articulating what "art" means in a Chinese context. We are "buds" or "sprouts" whose aim is to become "profound persons."

Imagination allows us to examine the possibilities that can lead to that end. To the degree that arts provide merely a "recovery of the same" (Alexander, 1987b, 6), they move in a direction opposed to that of art as experience. At their best, the arts crown the complex richness that is human experience. At their worst they distort experience, transforming it into the polarity of an antecedently fixed "subject" responding to stimuli emitted by the external world and its "objects."

Genuine, fully human, associations incline us toward the good when they manifest a fluid, vigorous participation in shared activities. One of the most important of these activities is a lively discussion about the nature and future of the society itself. Such a discussion can go on best when conditions for a shared social field are present. The work of nurturing this field is that of the arts. When they are flourishing, they bring us together, not as identical units, but as participants in shared endeavors. They help unite people within a social field where participation is encouraged. Social harmony is an important democratic ideal. It is the ultimate art work.

7

Devotion

Religious versus Religion

John Dewey wrote several short books. *Individualism Old and New* and *Experience and Education* are among the most prominent. Both of these, however, deal with topics that Dewey had treated in detail elsewhere. His small book on religion, *A Common Faith,* is an exception in this regard. It is his only sustained attempt at articulating a philosophy of religion. His other comments are brief and scattered.[1]

The paucity of texts may seem surprising for someone who, as a young man, began his classes with a fervent prayer (Dykhuizen, 25). It was disappointing for readers, religious or antireligious, who hoped for a comprehensive Deweyan statement on the level of James's *The Varieties of Religious Experience*, or Royce's *The Spirit of Christianity*. Reinhold Niebuhr registered his reservations by referring to the book as a "footnote," saying that it is "disappointing only in the sense that it is too brief to do full justice to the problem" (LW 9:453). A more recent commentator, generally sympathetic to Dewey, claims that he would be "inclined to place it below" Dewey's major works (Shea, 127).

Such readers think of the book as "thin" in depth as well as in size. Others are more appreciative. Charles Hartshorne credited Dewey with, perhaps inadvertently, developing a "theistic naturalism," a position identified by Hartshorne as the "twentieth century's supreme theoretical discovery" (Rockefeller, 526). The phrase "theistic naturalism" is richly ambiguous. To label Dewey a "naturalistic theist," implying that he accepted some form of traditional theism, would have been flatly incorrect. To label him a "religious naturalist," skirting the theism/atheism issue, would have been safe, but not nuanced enough for the position staked out by Dewey.

The expression "theistic naturalism," by contrast, indicates the challenge Dewey set for himself. He attempted to do something which was calculated to make neither friend nor foe of religion happy: Preserve a positive meaning for the term "religious," speak explicitly of "God," yet reject the beliefs of organized religion, including those in a supreme being antecedent to creation. This stance, as he admitted, situated him between "Wieman on the one hand and Corliss Lamont on the other," referring to the theologian Henry Nelson Wieman and the secular humanist Corliss Lamont (LW 9: 455).

Opponents on both sides of the issue would have preferred a definitive choice on Dewey's part. Several letters make clear, however, that Dewey accomplished just what he set out to do. In response to questions about *A Common Faith*, Dewey wrote the following to a soldier, Private Charles E. Witzell, in 1943.

> The lectures making up the book were meant for those whose religious beliefs had been abandoned, and who were given the impression that their abandonment left them without any religious beliefs whatever. I wanted to show them that religious values are not the monopoly of any one class or sect and are still open to *them*. (Anderson, 3)[2]

Similarly, in a letter to Max Otto, Dewey made clear that what he accomplished was exactly what he intended. "My book was written for the people who feel inarticulately that they have the essence of the religious with them and yet are repelled by the religions and are confused—primarily for them" (Rockefeller, 522).

The resulting formulations are replete with difficulties for an interpreter. Dewey is so focused on avoiding preexisting categories that the text is filled with subtle, often ambiguous, phrasings. This has led one commentator to conclude that the attempt to recover Dewey's meaning is an exercise in futility. "It is, I think, impossible to interpret them [Deweyan texts] in a way that will give them substance, force and life, without the fear that one is moving beyond Dewey and attributing ideas to him that he would deny" (LW 9:xxx). Nonetheless, Dewey does try to groom a new landscape within which fertile reflection on religion can thrive. An interrogation of his texts may indeed be exasperating, but it can provide some guidance for understanding him.

The obvious first question is to ask why Dewey wishes to preserve the "religious" while at the same time rejecting "religion." Why not admit that "religious" is an adjective associated with "religion" and that they stand or fall together? If the opposition between "religious values" and "religion" cannot, as Dewey insists, "be bridged" (LW 9:20), does this not mean that the "religious" should be retranslated into other terms with no remainder? Why confuse the issue, why not simply admit that both "religion" and the "religious" are irredeemably, hopelessly saturated with outdated and untenable connotations?

Dewey's refusal to be easily categorized in this respect seems to have been guided by a genuine feeling that the "religious" dimension of experience was both irreducible and commonly felt. The sort of experience he had in mind was simply not captured by alternative labels. There was some overlap between it and "moral" experience, and, especially, between it and "esthetic" experience. However, Dewey believed "religious" experience to be something more inclusive than these two. This is why he insisted on accommodating the term.

He needed a word connoting something that neither ethical nor aesthetic language could adequately encompass. To do this, he preserved the word "religious" in spite of the asomatic connotations that had come to be associated with the term. What Dewey had in mind was the fully inclusive, somatically integrated person who is motivated by an intense devotion, not just to individual well-being, nor to a combination of the good and the beautiful, but to "the sense of a connection of man, in the way of both dependence and support, with the enveloping world that the imagination feels is a universe" (LW 9:36). Acts engaged in by individuals who are mere specks on the cosmic scale can have an "infinite reach." Humans have this reach because the "small effort which we can put forth is in turn connected with an infinity of events that support it." This ideal, says Dewey, "is not a goal to be attained. It is a significance to be felt, appreciated" (MW14, 180). Such a "significance to be felt" is what Dewey has in mind when he chooses to admit the irreducibility of the "religious" as an experiential aspect of life.[3]

Dewey's position may be hard to classify, but it can be situated within the history of philosophy and understood as consistent with his own philosophical outlook. Taking the route of Galilean Purification, Kant had already attempted to pare down religion to what was acceptable in light of reason. The result was a desiccated apparatus where God and immortality were necessary postulates of morality. In effect, religion was reduced to a support for morality. Religion involved adherence to two existential claims, belief in deity and belief in immortality. There is little warmth in the Kantian position. This, coupled with Kant's continual emphasis on the individual who makes moral decisions in isolation, runs counter to Dewey's communitarian embrace of human life. He does not reiterate the Kantian position that posits transcendental foundations for ethics. Nonetheless, Dewey's understanding of the religious dimension of human experience is continuous with eighteenth-century critiques. He too accepts the inseparability of moral and religious concerns. The "religious" is a deeply felt, all inclusive sentiment that our efforts at securing a good life form part of a wider network (natural as well as social) which sustains those efforts.

As is often the case with Dewey, his approach combines Modern elements with some decidedly archaic, pre-Modern ones. The Modern elements involve accepting post-Enlightenment criticisms of religion. Like the cultures of premodernity, however, Dewey describes a situation in which the religious cannot be identified as one compartmentalized dimension of existence.

The Plotinian Temptation might lead us to seek out that single, "essential" activity identified by the word "religion." But this would be a decidedly Modern undertaking. Neither Hebrew nor classical Greek, for example, had separate words for religion. John Mbiti, in his discussion of African peoples, indicates that the same is true for many precolonial cultures. The absence of a specific term, ironically, may signal, not that the religious sensibility is absent, but that it is ubiquitous. "Africans," as Mbiti points out, were "notoriously religious" (Mbiti, 1). There is no word "religion" because there is no separate "thing" to be labelled as such. The religious character of life is all-pervasive. "Because traditional religions permeate all the departments of life, there is no formal distinction between the sacred and the secular, between the religious and the non-religious, between the spiritual and the material areas of life" (Mbiti, 2).

Whereas in contemporary cultures religion often resembles a club to which one gains admission, in traditional societies religion is all-encompassing. Dewey tends to use the word "religious" to capture some of this same pre-Modern breadth. He asserts that "it is of the nature of a religion based on the supernatural to draw a line between the religious and the secular and profane." His alternative, however, vitiates such distinctions. "The conception that 'religious' signifies a certain attitude and outlook, independent of the supernatural, necessitates no such division" (LW 9:45).

Dewey's aim is not to suggest that we go back in time. The same cultures that, in a positive sense, lived out the ubiquity of the religious as touching all dimensions of community life, were often, in a negative sense, closed to internal change and external influence. One was born into a culture and its religious practices. Personal choice was minimized, if not excluded altogether. Here is where modernity has made a definitive improvement. There may have been too great an emphasis on individualism in the Reformation, but this was a direction that needed to be taken (LW 9:45). Dewey does not seek to restore the past. He can be seen, however, as wanting to make vibrant once again certain pre-Modern attitudes, especially the pervasive nature of the religious dimension that marked societies like those described by Mbiti.

The philosopher cited as a model by Dewey is Spinoza. Here was someone who tried to hold together three important elements in the Western heritage: the Hebrew concern with righteousness, the Greek emphasis on intelligence, and the discoveries of the sciences (LW 4:45). Dewey's own synthesis goes beyond that of Spinoza in refusing to identify nature with God, and in coming to terms with twentieth- rather than seventeenth-century science. The aim, however, is similar, a generous synthesis that is inclusive in its embrace of religious values. Dewey does not move in the direction of an overintellectualized moralism. His analyses are meant to culminate in a sense of natural piety.

For a sense of natural piety to be recovered, the erroneous conception of religion, as a mode of knowledge competing with science, has to be rejected. The faith which is widespread, "common," is not the faith asserting that "some object or being exists as a truth for the intellect." It is, rather, one "that is a conviction that some end should be supreme over conduct" (LW 9: 15). This faith with a "moral and practical import" rather than a cognitive one, will anchor Dewey's views on the nature of the "religious."

The "Load" Carried by Traditional Religions

Before examining the constructive reformulations of "faith" presented by Dewey, it is important to examine the critique which prepares the clearing occupied by the faith with a "moral and practical import." The pre-Modern dimension of Dewey's thought reflects his desire for integration. The Modern dimension continues the Reformation aim of purgation. This project sought to scrape away the layers of adventitious accretions until an authentic core of religion was rediscovered.

Dewey's own New England had been especially active in this regard. From the Puritans to Emerson, the process of purification had followed a similar pattern. The Puritans jettisoned the last trappings of Catholicism in order to arrive at the purified inner core of religion. Their successors, the Unitarians, affected by the Enlightenment, emancipated religious belief from untenable intellectual commitments. Finally, Emerson and the transcendentalists continued the process, moving beyond what they considered to be the cold, overly rational approach of the Unitarians, and leaving behind entirely the world of organized religion.[4]

"The ideal factors in experience that may be called religious," Dewey says, must be sorted out from that "load of current beliefs and institutional practices that are irrelevant to them" (LW 9:8). The unique aspect of this project, in its Deweyan version, is that no core is found. There are no independent existences or events (God and immortality) that guarantee and ground morality. His proposal is not to outline a new, modified, more authentic, "religion," but to emancipate the "elements and outlooks that may be called religious" (LW 9:8).

A transcendentalist like Emerson is difficult to classify. He rejects religion, but he is not antireligious. Dewey's own approach to religion can best be situated within this tradition. Unlike Emerson, he was no transcendentalist. But, like Emerson, he articulated a position that refused preexistent categories. If Emerson is neither an adherent of religion nor a secularist, then neither is Dewey.

What is the "load" that Dewey wishes to jettison? There are specific intellectual commitments and ritualistic practices to be sure, but what Dewey mostly seeks is a reversal of traditional assumptions. Typically, religious practices and attitudes are said to be grounded or rooted in an absolute Being who is their source and guarantor. Dewey begins rather with practice and claims that, when certain conditions are met, the experience in question can be deemed "religious." We do not start with a divinity and then derive social practices. We start with social practices and when certain of them are infused with a conviction that their meaning is linked to wider natural and social forces, we come as close as is possible to what traditional religions had as best about them.

Faith

One of the positive legacies of modernity, in Dewey's view, was that of providing methods of inquiry for arriving at secure or warranted beliefs. As we have seen in chapter two, some of Dewey's labels for the newer methods of inquiry, "instrumentalism" and "pragmatism," brought unwanted connotations. This was also the case when Dewey praised science. He was thought to be embracing the "scientific method" and suggesting a treatment of social and moral issues via the particular techniques employed by physicists and chemists. Other formulations are less misleading. He refers to the method of "natural intelligence", "method of intelligence in action" (LW 9:51), or "new methods of inquiry and reflection" (LW 9:22). In each case, Dewey wishes to stress that warranted assertions result from inquiries that are (1) social, that is they are undertaken by a community of inquirers, and (2) can be justified by standards that are empirical.

Such methodological concerns are important with regard to religion. Too often, religions offer themselves as providing substitute, albeit nonverifiable, sources of knowledge. This, in turn, leads to acceptance of claims without examining them via the normal means of intellectual justification. Faith then becomes what it often is in popular consciousness, belief in the unbelievable.

W. K. Clifford (the person whom James answers in his famous essay "The Will to Believe") presented one possible response to the eagerness with which religious believers claimed access to unprovable truths. He asserted that humans would "sink back into savagery" if they lost their habits of "testing things and inquiring into them" (Clifford, 33). To avoid such backsliding, they must follow a simple rule: "it is wrong always, everywhere, and for anyone, to believe anything upon insufficient evidence" (Clifford, 34).

Clifford emphasized the criterion of "insufficient evidence" as a way of expunging religious beliefs. His case, however, was built on the irredeemably vague word, "insufficient." Dewey would certainly agree with Clifford on the importance of inquiry and the need for sufficient evidence as warranting belief. But Clifford, unlike Dewey, is still caught up in the "quest for certainty." "Those who do not have the time for exhaustive investigation," he concludes, "should have no time to believe" (Clifford, 34). Here is where the vagueness of "insufficient" becomes important. There is no fixed rule determining just how much evidence is "sufficient" and how much is "insufficient." An overly narrow construction of sufficiency, as argued for by Clifford, would paralyze most human agency.

Dewey's contextualism allows him to realize that the sufficiency or insufficiency of evidence is not based on a single, narrow scale. Rather, it is to be based on the sort of inquiry being undertaken, the kind of evidence available, and the amount of time at one's disposal. What counts as sufficient for a general in the midst of battle differs from what counts as sufficient for a farmer planning next year's crop, for a weather forecaster tracking a hurricane, or for an archaeologist examining a fragment of what was once a cooking utensil. If belief had to be denied whenever the evidence was "insufficient" in the narrow sense suggested by Clifford, then no one, not even Clifford himself, would select a career, or decide to wed. These important decisions are based on beliefs that cannot be guaranteed with absolute certainty. In itself, Clifford's formulation that belief should be suspended until time has been made for "exhaustive investigation," need not be problematic. However, it does become a source of practical paralysis if it is thought that one scale alone determines, acontextually, the level of investigation that defines "exhaustive."

By focusing on the centrality of practice, Dewey does not fear a more generous probabilism than is allowed by Clifford. The evidence must always be "sufficient," of course, but the very vagueness of the term can render it unhelpful. To redeem its use, the term must always be understood as relative to a context, to a purpose, and to the availability of time before a decision must be made. Human life is the province of probability and warranted beliefs. "Faith," on this account, need not be the automatically pejorative term that it was for antireligious thinkers like Clifford.

When we begin by emphasizing our daily circumstances, we realize quickly that the reach of apodictic proof is limited. What we ourselves have come to determine with exactitude is exceedingly narrow. Recognizing that the world of practice results from commitments linked to inquiries, Dewey admits that there is room for faith in his philosophical outlook. It is not a faith that forces one to believe in intellectual claims that have no support in evidence. It is rather a commitment that is practical in import. Dewey refers to it as a "moral" faith (LW 9:15).

The primacy of the "good" in Dewey's orientation takes on special importance here. He reacts against the asomatic understanding of humans as primarily thinking machines whose highest aim is to utter abstract truths. When humans are thought of as such disembodied "talking heads," faith is treated as a special intellectual faculty. Faith in religious pronouncements is then considered to be a way of accumulating truths beyond those warranted by accepted methods of intelligence. Religion and science become adversaries. But if humans are embodied, social creatures, turned fundamentally toward the good, then faith need not be an alternative to intelligent inquiry.

> Apart from any theological context, there is a difference between belief that is a conviction that some end should be supreme over conduct, and belief that some object or being exists as a truth for the intellect. Conviction in the moral sense signifies being conquered, vanquished, in our active nature by an ideal end; it signifies acknowledgment of its rightful claim over our desires and purposes. Such acknowledgment is practical, not primarily intellectual. (LW 9:15)

The two kinds of convictions distinguished by Dewey in this passage are significant with regard to his views on sorting out the "religious" from religion. One conviction is noetic. It is belief in a proposition asserting the existence of what cannot be supported by reasonable evidence, even when, *pace* Clifford, the standards of sufficiency are properly contextualized. Religion is thought to be one source of cognition, one which serves up facts via a process different from those of ordinary human intelligence. What this sort of faith adds is simply another pathway for accumulating information. So long as humans are primarily defined as minds aiming at truths, cognitive faith can keep religions alive by offering an attractive bonus: a special mode of access.

The other sort of conviction, the kind that is moral or practical, is concerned with flesh and blood human beings. We are not primarily "minds." Humans are embodied, active beings, aiming at the good. The elements combined by Dewey in the quotation play an important role here. He emphasizes our total, "active nature," with its "acknowledgment" of a conviction which guides our "desires" and "purposes."

Moral faith is an attitude that embraces the whole of our character. Instead of a belief that a particular object, or certain objects, exist, it is a belief in "the possibilities of nature and associated living," together with a "devotion to the ideal" (LW 4:242). It is a "sense of the whole" which "claims and dignifies" the "inconsequential acts of separate selves" (MW14, 227). Can we say with absolute certainty that such a faith is well placed? No, the quest for certainty is rejected outright. Are we committed with absolute rigidity to defend this feeling of integration with surrounding forces? No, infallibility and absolute commitment are idols which have found enough false worshippers in both the philosophical and religious communities. Is it nonetheless a justifiable commitment to the ideal harmony of natural and human forces? Dewey's answer is "Yes."

This sort of faith is rooted in ordinary life-experience. Human activity would simply be paralyzed if we had to answer Clifford-type criteria before committing to certain beliefs. We are not infallible computational machines pre-programmed with a single all-powerful algorithm. The evidence with which we are confronted is often partial, confused, and inconsistent. Our means of dealing with this data is not preset by any absolute formulae. Because of this we must make choices, commitments, acts of "faith," in the absence of absolute certainty. Dewey's "moral" faith, building on such a recognition, goes one step further. It is the conviction that in committing ourselves to seeking out the good, we are working, not in opposition to, but in conjunction with a complex of social and natural factors. "Faith," for Dewey, is not a term that needs to be rejected in its entirety. It is a concept that needs to be clarified. Cognitive faith is a pretender which should be dismissed. Moral faith, however, plays a central role in human life.

God

By the time Dewey composed *A Common Faith*, liberal theologians had experimented with a variety of formulations which would preserve belief in God's existence, but would eliminate both the problems of anthropomorphism in general, and the specific picturing of God as a harsh, judgmental father. Henry Nelson Wieman of the University of Chicago was one of the most prominent in this regard. It is said of him that he volunteered so many formulations that colleagues, seeing him on the campus, would ask "What are you calling it today, Henry?"

A more recent believer, John Macquarrie, claims that "the very fact that human beings do make commitments is itself some evidence for the reality of God." Commitments are acts of trust, and such trust, Macquarrie asserts, "rejects the belief that reality is cold, impersonal, mechanical, alien." "To entertain this basic trust," he continues, "is surely to give at least a minimal assent to part of what is meant by belief in God" (Macquarrie, 151). Here is the line that separates Dewey from believers. Dewey accepts "moral faith" and the sorts of commitments Macquarrie has in mind. He is even willing to discuss the "power of an ideal" as that of an "unseen power controlling our destiny" (LW 9:17). This, however, is as far as Dewey is willing to go.

In his discussion of Wieman's position, Dewey describes, not a line to be crossed, but a problematic shift made by the believer. "The shift is between the fact that men find conditions and forces in existence which generate and sustain the goods of living, and the assertion that these things constitute a unified and single object which '*rightly* demands the supreme devotion of all human living'" (LW 9:219). This is the step Dewey refuses to take. He accepts the description prior to the shift, but does not find any evidence for what follows it. The "conditions and forces" described by Wieman are "too universal and inclusive in human experience to be identified with any historic religious tradition whatever, to say nothing of Christian theism" (LW 9:220).

Wieman responded that Dewey failed "to follow through to the inevitable implications of his position" (Rockefeller, 525). In effect, he wanted to categorize Dewey as a "naturalistic theist." But Dewey remained steadfast. The error of theists, he believed, was to conflate the existence of "conditions and forces" with the existence of a single and unified being. The result: "something sufficiently 'jealous' and exclusive to be an emotional carrier of one strain of traditional religious belief" (LW 9:220). Like his model Spinoza, Dewey saw no need to go beyond nature to a separate being. "Nature, as the object of knowledge, is capable of being the source of constant good and a rule of life, and thus has all the properties and the functions which the Jewish-Christian tradition attributed to God" (LW 4:45).

The idea of a preexistent supernatural entity, source and end of human life, was simply rejected by Dewey. To say that it was simply rejected is the safest interpretation. He had little interest in following other philosophers such as Leibniz, Aristotle, Aquinas, or, his own contemporary, Whitehead, in undertaking a sustained examination of the question of God's existence. Philosophical arguments for or against the existence of God seem to have been of no concern to him. Theoretically, he felt that the movement of Modern science had discredited belief in an antecedent supreme being. Practically, his worry was that the traditional God, the jealous, punitive Father of the Puritan tradition, would always rear its head when discussions of God were introduced.

To accommodate these sentiments, one strategy would have been to eliminate altogether the term "God." Dewey could have developed a "religious naturalism" that refused all reference to the divine. But in *A Common Faith* he speaks explicitly of "God." This puzzling usage seems out of character. Why would Dewey, opponent of traditional theisms, signatory to the first *Humanist Manifesto*, refer to "God" in his most serious public reflections on religion? What is it in the term that leads Dewey to seek its preservation? Why is it that he formulates a position that would respond to Hartshorne's label "theistic naturalism?"

Two factors seem to be important here. The first is that in a transitional period, it is important to emphasize how a new position is not a complete rejection of that which went earlier. He rephrases a passage of Wieman to this effect.[5] The other, more significant, reason makes explicit just what needs to be preserved from the tradition. The rejection of the supernatural is too often accompanied by the temptation for humanity to place itself as the controlling force in the universe.

Utopians like the later H. G. Wells and the French thinker Charles Fourier tended to divinize humans as all-powerful creators, ever-perfectible beings whose ability to reshape a fully plastic world was unlimited. Dewey's naturalism, which accepts the immersion of human life within its natural ambient, is less likely to think in terms of "Men Like Gods," the title Wells gave to one of his books. Another post-theist tendency is best exemplified in Albert Camus's *The Rebel.* Here, the absence of God is taken to mean that the foundation for meaning has been removed from existence. The choices then become stark: acquiescence to the ultimate meaninglessness of life which, if followed out consistently, leads either to suicide or rebellion. The rebellion urged by Camus struggles against meaninglessness while admitting the ultimately futile nature of a quest for meaning in a world that is without a foundation for meaning.

Dewey rejects both the divinisation of humans and the need for rebellion. He emphasizes rather the sense of continuity with that conjunction of natural and social factors in which we are

imbedded. "Theistic naturalism" seeks to be an honest naturalism, appraising accurately the possibilities and limitations of
being human in this world. Neither the utopian nor the rebel is
sensitive enough to the importance of "dependence," an aspect of
the traditional view appreciated by Dewey.

> A religious attitude, however, needs the sense of a connec-
> tion of man, in the way of both dependence and support,
> with the enveloping world that the imagination feels is a
> universc. Use of the words "God" or "divine" to convey the
> union of actual with ideal may protect man from a sense of
> isolation and from consequent despair or defiance. (LW
> 9:36)[6]

Overemphasis on the Promethean powers of humanity, in fact, is
the new danger posed by the rejection of traditional religions.
"A humanistic religion, if it excludes our relation to nature, is
pale and thin, as it is presumptuous, when it takes humanity as
its object of worship" (LW 9:36).

Humans must constantly be reminded that they depend on
forces which are outside of them. Both traditional theism and
"aggressive atheism" share the mistaken assumption of treating
"man in isolation." Traditional theism recognizes the importance
of dependence, but errs in formulating the dependence as that of
an isolated individual on a preexistent God. The reaction of atheism too often rejects not only the divine but all sense of dependence. It is this dual rejection that Dewey wishes to reconsider.

Properly understanding the human condition means recognizing our dependence on factors which we did not create.
Humans are like artists. They work both within the limitations
imposed by the materials, and extend the possibilities of that
material beyond what had initially been given. Given this context,
a philosopher may continue to use the word "God." Humans
understood as artists of the good are sustained by a faith in the
consistency of their aspirations with the multiplicity of natural
forces within which they are imbedded. For Dewey, this identifies
a faith in what can be called "God."

> But this idea of God, or of the divine, is also connected with
> all the natural forccs and conditions—including man and
> human association—that promote the growth of the ideal
> and that further its realization. . . . For there are forces in

> nature and society that generate and support the ideals. They are further unified by the action that gives them coherence and solidity. It is this *active* relation between ideal and actual to which I would give the name "God." I would not insist that the name *must* be given. (LW 9:34)

Dewey admits that it is not necessary to preserve the word "God." However, he chooses to do so. This is because the word serves two important functions: (1) It minimizes the tendency to divinize human beings, and (2) it highlights the variety of forces that must work together if the good is to be realized in the world.

Dewey's highest ideal is, as we have seen, "Good" rather than "God." But, as he realizes, there is not only an etymological relationship between the two terms. That reality which came to be associated with a specific sort of supernatural entity was, for him, the totality of factors, human and nonhuman, which, when properly directed, can issue in the realization of concrete goods. The name God must no longer be reserved for a preexisting ideal, a fixed, unchanging entity. Rather, consistent with Dewey's overall focus, the term is now reserved for the functioning, participatory activities that make concrete goods come to life in actual conditions.

What results is a position hard to classify. Dewey is certainly an antitheist. Without much philosophical discussion he simply assumes that the advances of modernity have made obsolete any belief in the supernatural being worshipped by religions. He is also, as the word is usually understood, a-theistic. Here, though, clear-cut formulations can be misleading. *A Common Faith* does redefine the notion of divinity and preserve the term "God." It also promulgates an attitude identified by its author as "religious." Wieman, himself, in reviewing Dewey's book, began by saying that "some of us have known for a long time that he (Dewey) was a deeply religious man" (LW 9:426).

Since the word "atheistic" carries with it connotations of being also irreligious, applying that label to Dewey could lead to an oversimplified interpretation of his position. As Steven Rockefeller points out in his detailed study of Dewey's views on religion, "Dewey never referred to himself as an atheist and did not like being labelled one. He felt that the word 'atheism' carries negative connotations that do not accurately characterize his worldview" (Rockefeller, 519). Nor was Dewey a proselytizer bent on converting people away from their faiths. His 1943 letter to

Charles Witzell makes a point of saying that "I have taught many years and I don't think that any students would say that I set out to undermine anyone's faith" (Anderson, 3). Considerations such as these help us understand why neither the word "theist" nor "atheist" in their full-blown connotations was suitable for Dewey.

Such a complex result is not unusual for empirical naturalism. As we discussed in the previous chapter, Dewey rejected the Modern myth, given one articulation in Descartes's *Discourse*, that the structures of the past would have to be completely razed before new philosophical edifices could be erected. His attitude in this respect was more like that of Aristotle in relation to his predecessors. Earlier thinkers need to be improved upon, but this does not mean that their ideas have to be erased entirely. Their flaws were due to a limited or partial grasp of things. Strands of thought from the tradition are not to be automatically rejected. Properly mended, they can be woven into a new intellectual cloth.

Cooperation

The culminating point of the religious attitude for Dewey is the sense of cooperative participation signalled by "God," "the unity of all ideal ends arousing us to desire and actions" (LW 9:29). Deweyan naturalism is ample and honest enough to make room for "natural piety." "Awe" and "reverence" rest "upon a sense of human nature as a cooperating part of a larger whole." The piety which is based on the sense of humans as intelligent participants in the wider natural milieu, "is an inherent constituent of a just perspective in life" (LW 9:18). Dewey is willing to use words like "awe," "reverence," and "piety" because they describe common experiences. The "religious" aspect which permeates lives is a "comprehensive attitude," one which "is much broader than anything indicated by 'moral' in its usual sense" (LW 9:17).

What Dewey wishes to preserve is a sense of cooperating with forces beyond those created by human choice. Greek philosophers had held three forces in tension: the supernatural, the natural, and the human. Post-Renaissance thought, Modern thought, as it progressed, evolved toward an ever more pronounced anthropocentrism. Humans became the center, eliminating the supernatural, and dreaming of dominating the natural.

Dewey often succumbs to the anthropocentric temptation.[7] At other times, as in *A Common Faith*, this tendency is mitigated. Here, Dewey is sensitive to the excesses which result from an overemphasis on will, and a transformation of nature into sheer plasticity. Fantasies and utopias litter the intellectual landscape of the nineteenth and twentieth centuries. The natural world of which we are a part, and within which we undertake our life journey, is neither mere stuff awaiting human manipulation, nor is it a mere temptation to be fled. Dewey's reformulation of the ancient triad of supernatural, natural, and human is articulated so that the three forces remain, although they are considerably redefined.

> But this idea of God, or of the divine, is also connected with all the natural forces and conditions—including man and human association—that promote the growth of the ideal and that further its realization. . . . For there are forces in nature and society that generate and support the ideals. (LW 9:34)

Ultimately, for Dewey, "religious" conveys the awareness of a conjunction of forces that, when cooperating, can bring about a transformation in life. It is not an attitude restricted to the "moral" concerns in the life of a community. The "religious" reaches beyond this to a grasp made possible via a genuinely experience-based naturalism. Such a naturalism welcomes the embodied imagination (not the autonomous, unbridled faculty of utopians) as the capacity to grasp possibilities offered by, but not realized in, our immediate surroundings. An experience that is "religious" culminates in a sense of integration given to us via the more inclusive grasp made possible by imaginative extension.

> Hence the idea of a thoroughgoing and deep-seated harmonizing of the self with the Universe (as a name for the totality of conditions with which the self is connected) operates only through imagination—which is one reason why this composing of the self is not voluntary in the sense of an act of special volition or resolution. (LW 9:14)

The "harmony of the self with the Universe" does not result from wishful thinking. It is not simply a choice willed into existence by "an act of special volition." It is a projection beyond the immediate, but rooted in it. It is something to be felt and appreciated. As one of Dewey's most prominent pupils, John Herman Randall Jr., put it, when we commit ourselves to a "supreme good," we are "cooperating with what is most real in the universe" (Randall, 74).

One reason why Dewey may have hesitated to follow modernity's drive toward complete secularization was an experience he had in the years immediately after college, while he was teaching in Oil City, Pennsylvania. He referred to it as "mystical." The experience, as Steven Rockefeller interprets it, "was a blissful experience in which his worries and fears seemed to fall away and he was filled with a sense of deep trust and oneness with the universe" (Rockefeller, 67).[8]

Dewey was convinced that such a "religious" sensibility was not at all uncommon among human beings. Religions with their dogmas had tried to intellectualize it, to make it a rival to science. But the sense of being led on by the unseen, of being part of a network of cooperating forces, was, he believed a "common" occurrence. "Many a person" had achieved "without presumption and without display, such unification of themselves and of their relations to the conditions of existence." What Dewey's little book sought to do was to extend the spirit and inspiration of such individuals to "ever wider numbers" (LW 9:19).

8

Conclusion

Postmodern or Polytemporal?

Dewey's formative years spanned the period from the Civil War to the Treaty of Versailles. Recognizing the tremendous changes that have taken place since that time, we, entering the twenty-first century, might be tempted to treat Dewey as a historical curiosity, not as a living presence in the philosophical conversation. The contemporary intellectual climate, captivated as it is by postmodernism, encourages not only moving beyond the past, but also skepticism toward any systematic thinker.[1] The hermeneutics of suspicion seems to have triumphed decisively over the hermeneutics of recovery.

One reason for writing this book, an attempt at a hermeneutics of recovery, is that Dewey's mode of dealing with his intellectual ancestry challenges the whole notion of thinking in terms of pre-Modern, Modern, and post-Modern. The French philosopher Michel Serres has argued that, in spite of the Modern penchant to view time as divided into neat epochs, each era is and ought to aim at being "multitemporal" (Serres, 92). Our quest should be to absorb and update what is best from the past, adjust its misplaced emphases, eliminate its errors, and incorporate novel elements needed to address our own time.

The resulting synthesis would be under no compulsion to make a fetish of overcoming the past. There is no need, as Bruno Latour points out, to continue the "lost flight of post-post-post modernists" (Latour, 69). Those who claim to be doing something radically new, Serres indicates insightfully, are engaging in self-promotion, using the language of Madison Avenue (Serres, 211). Serious philosophy, by contrast, should not be tempted by such self-promotion. Instead, its work involves seizing and struggling with important issues facing its own time. Success in this endeavor requires one to take Peirce's admonition seriously: "do not block the way of inquiry" (Peirce, 54). In turn, this admonition requires an inclusive attitude, one that avoids *a priori* exclusions, and makes no fetish about absolute novelty.

To think in terms of a multitemporal synthesis for the present relieves philosophy from a temptation to which it regularly succumbs: playing the part of a prosecutor engaged primarily in "critique" and "denunciation" (Latour, 64). Hegel had described the task of philosophy as that of arriving at the actual cognizance "of what truly is" (Hegel, 46). For Hegel "what truly is" was inseparable from what had been. The present could not be understood without realizing how it grew out of and absorbed what had preceded it. Keeping this Hegelian sensitivity to temporal continuity, while offering a more prosaic formulation, I would claim that the task for philosophers is to *think our own time*. Once we abandon the quest for radical rupture, we can, as Dewey did, formulate a comprehensive scheme to "think our own time."

Given that Dewey's way of dealing with philosophical issues rejects *a priori* exclusions, it is not surprising that, like Plato, he makes no sharp bifurcation between *logos* and *mythos*. "Philosophic discourse partakes both of scientific and literary discourse. Like literature, it is a comment on nature and life in the interest of a more intense and just appreciation of the meaning present in experience" (LW 1:304).[2] Although Dewey, unlike Plato, has not invented stories of his own, he describes his work as a kind of narrative. If we wish to inhabit a "cosmos," not a world that is "chaos," we must articulate a "composed tale of meanings" (MW 13:279). "Why be as the dumb beasts which perish," he asks, "when events so alluringly invite us to tell that story about them which wise men have called truth and art?" (MW 13:280). Telling such a "story" is what Dewey attempted. The characters in this story are flesh and blood human beings. The scene is the life-world in the fullness disclosed via experience. The plot is that of identifying, establishing, and securing goods of all kinds. The means are the multiple arts (which include the sciences)[3] and a common faith.

Dewey's Relevance

Dewey's distance from us means that we cannot agree with all that he says. Nonetheless, he can speak to us anew. Dialogue with him can bear fruit as we face the contemporary challenge of providing our own "tale of meanings." Any such tale will include the elements addressed by Dewey: a concrete grasp of the life-world, an understanding of human intelligence, the articulation of social ideals, the place of education, integration of the arts, and the proper role for devotion and commitment.

In addition, Dewey is worth listening to because the twentieth century is ending on several notes that refocus our attention on themes he made prominent. More than ever we recognize the reach of interconnection, interdependence, and interaction. Decisions made about oil supplies in Nigeria, construction of a blue jean factory in China, the rate of inflation in the United States, these all have repercussions far beyond national boundaries. Ecologists keep reminding us that our interactions with the natural world are as important as interactions between ourselves. The life-world is not a scene of isolated agents. It is, as Dewey emphasized, one dominated by interconnections and interdependencies.

The last decades of the twentieth century have also witnessed an upsurge in democratic aspirations. Whether it is the fall of communism in Europe or the successes of popularly elected governments in Latin America, indications point to a deep desire among people to live in democratic societies. The crucial philosophical questions, "what is democracy," "what are its central ideals," and "how are these to be woven together in an effective synthesis," thus take on a new urgency. As we ask these questions anew, Dewey can serve as one of the foremost twentieth-century sources of inspiration.

Such considerations indicate that the terrain he prepared is that within which we continue to toil. As we undertake to work the landscape we have inherited, two procedures that Dewey warned against still need to be avoided. One is simply to "revive the 'classics.'" The other is to do no more than echo the currents of the day, to "become extreme modernists" (MW 13:278). As I have tried to show in this study, Dewey's own trajectory was "polytemporal" (I borrow this formulation which mixes Greek and Latin etymology, thus being polychronic itself, from Bruno Latour, 102). Dewey sought to incorporate the best aspirations and attitudes from both the Modern and the pre-Modern, while correcting their deficiencies. This blend he combined with contemporary discoveries in order to address the cluster of issues specific to his own time.

My study of this endeavor has been sympathetic because I believe that the Deweyan landscape is one within which we can

FIGURE 8.1

John Dewey's Ninetieth Birthday Celebration,
New York Waldorf Astoria Hotel, 1949

John Dewey and (left to right): Cricket Rogers (back turned to the camera), Susan Rogers, Carry MacFadden, Toni Graham, Johnny Dewey, Jr., Roberta L. Dewey, Helen Potts (behind Roberta), and Adrienne Dewey. Courtesy of John Dewey Papers, Special Collections/Morris Library, Southern Illinois University at Carbondale.

reap a rich intellectual harvest. This does not mean that we should transform him into a "classic" to be copied exactly. Such a move, indeed, would be radically un-Deweyan. It would ignore time, context, and change. It would also not recognize the weaknesses in Dewey's philosophy. Those have been addressed amply by his critics: he was too dependent on science, too optimistic, too anthropocentric. In addition, the "personal" dimension is lacking from his thought. Nowhere does he address in any detail the issues made prominent by existentialist thinkers: love, friendship, death, and suffering.

Such limitations notwithstanding, Dewey did what all good philosophers do. He succeeded in leaving a large and fertile legacy. My attempt in this book has been to highlight those Deweyan plant stocks that can continue to be helpful in the hybridization necessary for our own time. If I have been successful, readers will want to turn to Dewey's texts themselves. Those wishing to do so would be well advised to begin with the works highlighting "experience" in the title: *Experience and Nature*, *Experience and Education*, and *Art as Experience*. My own view is that the reader who begins there will find a richer vein of material to carry over into the twenty-first century than one who begins with Dewey's logical works such as *How We Think* or *Logic: The Theory of Inquiry*. Beginning with the latter has two drawbacks. The first is that to use them as a starting point reinforces the attitude that epistemological concerns are the main issues dealt with by philosophers, a position which Dewey, as we have seen, specifically rejected. Second, Dewey's logical works reveal him as still overly influenced by the Cartesian fascination with "method." They provide the source of formulations, which if read uncritically, mislead commentators into claiming that the "pragmatic interpretation of knowledge as an instrument of adaptation and control implied that only scientific inquiry generated knowledge about the nature of the world" (Sidorsky, xvii). In fact, as we saw in chapter 2, Dewey specifically rejects such a narrow access to knowledge. The texts with "experience" in their titles offer a better introduction because they situate us directly and multidimensionally within the life-world.

Dewey was a complex thinker who held together many strands that we might no longer think blend particularly well. As we move into the twenty-first century we must choose which strands to emphasize and which to leave behind. My own effort has been to understand Dewey via the filter of organic metaphors. Life, living systems, cells, adaptation, these provide fruitful ways of highlighting the sides of Dewey that I believe are important as we begin the new century.[4] Of course, these are "root-metaphors"[5] that Dewey shares with Aristotle, Leibniz, and Whitehead. But that fact should not be disturbing. After all, a vibrant philosophy will always be polytemporal.

Appendix A:
Biographical Data

The only comprehensive biography of Dewey's extraordinarily long and eventful life is by George Dykhuizen. Neil Coughlan's study is exemplary but only takes Dewey to the Chicago years. Stephen Rockefeller, Robert Westbrook and Alan Ryan weave Dewey's life and thought together in their important studies.

1859   20 October, birth of John Dewey, Burlington, Vermont
1875   Enters University of Vermont
1879   Graduates from university
1879   Begins two years of high school teaching in Oil City, Pennsylvania
1882   Winter term, high school teacher, Charlotte, Vermont
1882   "The Metaphysical Assumptions of Materialism" appears in *The Journal of Speculative Philosophy*
1882   Begins graduate study at the Johns Hopkins University Influenced especially by the neo-Hegelian George Sylvester Morris, takes courses with Charles S. Peirce
1884   Joins the University of Michigan faculty
1886   28 July, marries Alice Chipman
1888   Joins University of Minnesota faculty
1889   Returns to the University of Michigan, replacing George Morris
1894   Joins the University of Chicago faculty, appoints George Herbert Mead to the department
1894   Son Morris, two and a half years old, dies of diptheria on a trip to Italy
1895   Opening of the "University Elementary School," also known as the "Dewey School" or the "Laboratory School"
1904   5 April, Dewey resigns from the University of Chicago after the university's failure to appoint his wife permanent principal of the Laboratory School
1904   Son Gordon, eight years old, dies of typhoid on a trip to England and Ircland

1905	1 February, Dewey joins the Columbia University faculty
1915	Helps found the American Association of University Professors
1919	February and March, Dewey lectures at the Imperial University of Tokyo, subsequently published as *Reconstruction in Philosophy*
1919–1920	Lectures in China
1920	Receives honorary degree from the National University, citation calls him the "Second Confucius"
1922	Delivers the Carus Lectures, subsequently published as *Experience and Nature*
1924	Visits Turkey and prepares a report on the Turkish Educational System
1927	Alice Dewey dies
1928	Visits Soviet Union, on his return writes a series of laudatory articles about Soviet education
1929	Delivers Gifford Lectures at the University of Edinburgh, subsequently published as *The Quest for Certainty*
1930	Retires from Columbia University, is appointed Professor Emeritus of Philosophy in Residence
1930	Receives honorary degree from the Sorbonne
1931	Delivers the William James Lectures at Harvard, subsequently published as *Art as Experience*
1932	Receives honorary degree from Harvard
1934	Delivers the Terry Foundation Lectures at Yale, subsequently published as *A Common Faith.*
1935	The John Dewey society is founded by a group of educators
1937	Serves as chairman of the commission of inquiry to investigate Soviet charges against Leon Trotsky
1946	Marries Roberta Lowitz Grant
1951	Receives an honorary degree from Yale
1952	1 June, dies in his New York City apartment from pneumonia

The ashes of John and Roberta Dewey are buried beside the chapel at the University of Vermont.

Appendix B:
Dewey in Cyberspace

The online discussion group devoted to Dewey's philosophy is one of the most cordial on the internet. It was begun by Todd Lekan, now at Muskingum College. It is presently managed by Tom Burke at the University of South Carolina. To join the discussion send the message listed below to the listserv address.

Message: subscribe jdewey-l firstname lastname
Address: listserv@vm.sc.edu

The Center for Dewey Studies, directed by Larry Hickman at Southern Illinois University, has its own homepage: http://www.siu.edu/~deweyctr. In addition to being a source for activities at the Dewey Center, this homepage is valuable for its list of the latest secondary literature on Dewey.

Craig Cunningham at Northeastern Illinois University has set up a comprehensive homepage which includes a section on Dewey: http://www.ecnet.net/users/uccunnin/index.html.

The Institute for Learning Technologies at Columbia University also has several sites relating to Dewey:

http://www.ilt.columbia.edu/academic/digittexts/dewey/bio.dewey

http://www.ilt.columbia.edu/academic/texts/dewey/d_e/contents.html

The writings of Dewey are also available on CD-ROM:

Hickman, Larry, ed. (1996). *The Collected Works of John Dewey: The Electronic Edition.* Charlottesville, VA: Intelex Corp.

Notes

Introduction

1. Cf. The comments of Marcel Mauss: "Moreover, among American philosophers, he [Dewey] is one whom Durkheim put ahead of all the others, and it is a great regret of mine not to have been able to attend the last great philosophy lecture of Durkheim, dedicated in great part to Professor Dewey" (LW 5:500–501).

2. When George Raymond Geiger wrote a book about Dewey for the centennial of the latter's birth, he felt obliged to begin with a caveat about his subject's waning influence: "This is a peculiar time in which to be writing about John Dewey. It is a time when almost every fundamental part of his philosophy seems to have been rejected" (Geiger, 3). Robert Westbrook's magisterial study of Dewey's political philosophy recently echoed the same theme: "At the time of his death, Dewey's influence as a philosopher, educator, and democrat was approaching its nadir" (Westbrook, 537).

3. See the titles in the bibliography, especially those by Westbrook, Rockefeller, Alexander, Boisvert, West, Hickman, Gouinlock, Ryan, Tiles, Campbell and Shusterman.

4. The main accusation against Dewey was that his position often slid over the line between justifiable hope and an overly optimistic utopianism that failed to appreciate the inherent flaws in the human condition. So prominent a supporter of Dewey as John McDermott has voiced the criticism directly: "Unfortunately he [Dewey] had an undeveloped doctrine of evil, the demonic, and the capacity of human beings *en masse* to commit heinous crimes against other human beings" (LW 11:xxxii). Alan Ryan similarly complains that "it was the role of brute power that Dewey could never quite reconcile himself to" (Ryan, 295). My own development of this criticism can be found in "The Nemesis of Necessity: Tragedy's Challenge to Deweyan Pragmatism," in David Seiple, ed. *Democracy and the Aesthetics of Intelligence: New Essays in Deweyan Reconstruction* (Albany: SUNY Press, forthcoming 1997). Most criticisms of Dewey revolve around this central charge of neglecting the inevitable tendency to evil in human beings. As a result, critics claim, Dewey voiced an overly sanguine hope in solving human problems via

the method of intelligence alone, he overemphasized the role of education in shaping character, and too glibly skimmed over the human tendency to self-interest and egoism. Works of critics who have challenged
Dewey in these regards can be found in the bibliography. See the bibli-
ographic entries for Reinhold Niebuhr, Ernest Gellner, and John Patrick
Diggins.

5. A thinker deeply influenced by Dewey, Irwin Edman, echoed
the Deweyan sentiment with characteristic lucidity. "'Under whatever
sky I had been born, since it is the same sky, I should have had the
same philosophy.' Nothing could better express than this sentence of
Santayana's the ambition and the illusion of the philosophic mind, the
aspiration to survey the scene of nature and of life with such candor and
exactness that the prejudices of time, place, and temperament will vanish and that the thoughts one speaks will be the thoughts of Nature her-
self. I have no such illusion. I know I speak here and now . . . amidst the
distractions of New York, and in the society somehow commonly known
as academic solitude" (Edman, 17).

6. "Greek polytheism, surprisingly, articulates a certain element of
Kantian morality better than any monotheistic creed could: namely, it
insists upon the supreme and binding authority, the divinity so to
speak, of *each* ethical obligation, in all circumstances whatever, including those in which the gods themselves collide" (Nussbaum, 49).

7. Stephen Toulmin has touched on the Dewey/Wittgenstein connection in his introduction to volume 4 of Dewey's Collected works, *The
Quest for Certainty*. See Toulmin, xii–xiii.

8. After discussing the physiological imagery that is pervasive in
Greek tragedians, Ruth Padel makes this comment on Greek dualism:
"When I speak of innards, I mean all this equipment of feeling and
thinking. The poets treat these words fluidly as organs, vessels, liq-
uid, breath. But I am not suggesting that tragedians 'blurred' distinctions we make between mind and body, or that these words were
ambiguous, or that the psychological 'overlapped' the physical in
Greek thought. These critical metaphors of blur and overlap would
imply that the Greeks perceived two different things to blur, two
meanings to slip between. If the distinctions and meanings are ours,
not theirs, then there were no two things for them to blur or to be
ambiguous about. It is not useful to project semantic fields of our own
words, like heart, soul, mind, or spirit, or to talk in terms of slippage"
(Padel, 39).

9. Alan Ryan, explaining why Dewey has once again become fash-
ionable, claims that the 1990s "are turning out to be astonishingly like
the 1890s" (Ryan, 24).

1. The Life-World

1. See Peirce's essay "Some Questions Concerning Certain Faculties Claimed for Man," in *Collected Papers of Charles Sanders Peirce*, vol. 5, ed. Charles Hartshorne and Paul Weiss (Cambridge, Mass.: Harvard University Press, 1934.

2. On Dewey's use of "growth" see *Democracy and Education* (MW 9), chapter 4 "Education as Growth" and chapter 5, "Preparation, Unfolding, and Formal Discipline," and Dewey's contribution to the *Encyclopaedia and Dictionary of Education*, MW 13:402.

3. See the bibliography for data on Burtt's essay.

4. Cf. "Our constant and unescapable concern is with prosperity and adversity, success and failure, achievement and frustration, good and bad. Since we are creatures with lives to live, and find ourselves within an uncertain environment, we are constructed to note and judge in terms of bearing upon weal and woe—upon value" (LW 1:33).

2. Thinking

1. "The discipline termed Epistemology assumes rightly or wrongly, a self-enclosed island of mind on one side, individual and private and only private; over against this is set a world of objects which are physically or cosmically there—and only there. Then it is naturally worried about how the mind can get out of itself to know a world beyond, or how the world out there can creep into 'consciousness'" (MW 6:18).

2. "Literally of course, 'epistemology' means only the theory of knowledge; the term *might* therefore have been employed simply as a synonym for a descriptive logic; for a theory that takes knowledge as it finds it and attempts to give the same kind of an account of it that would be given of any other natural function or occurrence. But the mere mention of what *might* have been only accentuates what is. The things that pass for epistemology all assume that knowledge is not a natural function or event, but a mystery. . . . Hence the primary problem of epistemology is: How is knowledge *uberhaupt*, knowledge at large, *possible?*" (MW 3:119).

3. "Even such new movements as pragmatism and instrumentalism already have their accretion of myths which stand in place of the ideas themselves. Probably the unfortunate names themselves invite the creation and encourage the spread of these myths" (LW 3:145).

4. Cf. "The world picture does not change from an earlier medieval one into a modern one, but rather the fact that the world becomes a picture at all is what distinguishes the essence of the modern age" (Heidegger, 130). See also Burnyeat, and Jonas.

5. Cf. "That the significance of the words, "subject" and "object" has undergone reversal in the history of philosophic thought is a well-known fact. What we call "objects" were in Greek terminology *subjects*; they were existences taken in their status as *subject*-matter of knowledge. Their logical forms were determined by the basic division supposed to exist in Nature between the changing and the eternal. Things that change are too unstable to be subjects of knowledge in its exact and complete sense. *Knowledge* as distinct from sense and opinion is fixed; truth does not alter. Hence the subjects ("objects" in our "sense") must also be invariable" (LW 12:88–89).

6. For a more detailed treatment of this terminological reversal, see my *Dewey's Metaphysics*, pp. 72–90.

7. "As *undergoing* inquiry, the material has a different logical import from that which it has as the *outcome* of inquiry. In its first capacity and status it will be called by the general name *subject-matter*. . . . The name *objects* will be reserved for subject-matter so far as it has been produced and ordered in settled form by means of inquiry; proleptically, objects are the *objectives* of inquiry (LW 12:122).

8. Cf. "Knowledge is still regarded by most thinkers as a direct grasp of ultimate reality, although the practice of knowing has been assimilated to the procedure of the useful arts;—involving, that is to say, doing that manipulates and arranges natural energies" (LW 1:268).

9. "What has been said helps to explain why the term 'warranted assertion' is preferred to the terms *belief* and *knowledge*. It is free from the ambiguity of these latter terms, and it involves reference to inquiry as that which warrants assertion" (LW 12:15).

10. Cf. "The meaning of the Copernican reversal is that we do not have to go to knowledge to obtain an exclusive hold on reality. The world as we experience it is a real world. But it is not in its primary phases a world that is known, that is understood, and is intellectually coherent and secure. Knowing consists of operations that give experienced objects a form in which the relations, upon which the onward course of events depends, are securely experienced. It marks a transitional redirection and rearrangement of the real. It is intermediate and instrumental; it comes between a relatively casual and accidental experience of existence and one relatively settled and defined" (LW 4:236–36),

3. Democracy

1. Explaining "pragmatism" as rooted in the thought of Charles S. Peirce, Dewey says the following. "Thus the theory of Peirce is opposed to every restriction of the meaning of a concept to the achievement of a particular end, and still more to a personal aim. It is still more strongly opposed to the idea that reason or thought should be reduced to being a servant of any interest which is pecuniary or narrow. This theory was American in origin in so far as it insisted on the necessity of human conduct and the fulfillment of some aim in order to clarify thought. But at the same time, it disapproves of those aspects of American life which make action an end in itself, and which conceive ends too narrowly and too 'practically'" (LW 2:6–7).

2. "But the rise of machine-industry, controlled by finance-capitalism, was a force that was not taken into account. It gave liberty of action to those particular natural endowments and individuals that fitted into the new economic picture. Above all, the Industrial Revolution gave scope to the abilities involved in acquiring property and to the employment of that wealth in further acquisitions. The employment of these specialized acquisitive abilities has resulted in the monopoly of power in the hands of the few to control the opportunities of the wide masses and to limit their free activities in realizing their natural capacities" (LW 11:369–370).

3. In *Human Nature and Conduct* Dewey complained that prefixing "self" to certain terms distorts what positive sense they originally had. "Many good words get spoiled when the word self is prefixed to them: Words like pity, confidence, sacrifice, control, love" (MW 14:96). In the 1932 *Ethics* he explicitly warned that "to make self-realization a conscious aim might and probably would prevent full attention to those very relationships which bring about the wider development of the self" (LW 7:302).

4. "If the early liberals had put forth their special interpretation of liberty as something subject to historic relativity they would not have frozen it into a doctrine to be applied at all times under all social circumstances" (LW 11:27).

5. For a more detailed critique of freedom as autonomy, see my "Heteronomous Freedom."

6. Cf. "Superiority and inferiority are meaningless words taken by themselves. They refer to some specific outcome. No one should use the words until he has asked himself and is ready to tell others: Superior or inferior in *what*?" (MW 13:296).

7. "The doctrine of equality never meant what some of its critics supposed it to mean. It never asserted equality of natural gifts. It was a moral, a political and legal principle, not a psychological one" (LW 13:108).

4. The Public

1. Ortega argues in this book that two principles above all others have shaped recent European life: liberal democracy and technological knowledge. "Such an overwhelming fact forces us, unless we prefer not to use our reason, to draw these conclusions: first, that liberal democracy based on technical knowledge is the highest type of public life hitherto known; secondly, that type may not be the best imaginable, but the one we imagine as superior to it must preserve the essence of those two principles; and thirdly, that to return to any forms of existence inferior to that of the XIXth Century is suicidal" (Ortega y Gasset, 52).

2. The best discussion of democratic realism and its Deweyan response are found in Westbrook. The author signifies his sympathies early on by saying that "Dewey's democratic theory retains a measure of importance for those like myself who are dissatisfied with the limited vision of democratic realism" (Westbrook, xvi–xvii).

3. "The private citizen interested in some cause would belong, as he does now, to voluntary societies which employed a staff to study the documents, and make reports that served as a check on officialdom. There would be some study of this material by newspaper men, and a good deal by experts and by political scientists. But the outsider, and every one of us is an outsider to all but a few aspects of modern life, has neither time, nor attention, nor interest, nor equipment for specific judgment. It is on the men inside, working under conditions that are sound, that the daily administrations of society must rest" (Lippmann, 1965, 251).

5. Educating

1. Cp. Alan Ryan's comments: "Dewey himself argued that it was not enough to repudiate traditional education. As he had remarked of the relationship between atheism and traditional religion, the trouble with mere opposition is that we are excessively influenced by what we negate. It was not enough for progressive teachers to throw out everything the old schools had done, to replace discipline by chaos, a rigid syllabus with no syllabus. And Dewey was inclined to think that many schools had done exactly that and had used his name to justify it" (Ryan, 282).

2. "Cooking may be so taught that it has no connection with country life, and with the sciences that find their unity in geography. Perhaps it generally has been taught without these connections being really made. But all the materials that come into the kitchen have their origin in the country; they come from the soil, are nurtured through the influences of light and water, and represent a great variety of local environments. Through this connection, extending from the garden into the larger world, the child has his most natural introduction to the study of the sciences" (MW 1:50).

3. "School facilities must be secured of such amplitude and efficiency as will in fact and not simply in name discount the effects of economic inequalities, and secure to all the wards of the nation equality of equipment for their future careers. Accomplishment of this end demands not only adequate administrative provision of school facilities, and such supplementation of family resources as will enable youth to take advantage of them, but also such modifications of traditional ideals of culture, traditional subjects of study and traditional methods of teaching and discipline as will retain all the youth under educational influences until they are equipped to be masters of their own economic and social careers" (MW 9:104).

6. Making

1. The term's origin is to be found in Alexander Baumgarten's *Reflections on Poetry*, 1735, p. 78.

2. "The Greeks and Romans had no conception of what we call art as something different from craft; what we call art they regarded merely as a group of crafts, such as the craft of poetry (*ars poetica*), which they conceived, sometimes no doubt with misgivings, as in principle just like carpentry and the rest, and differing from any one of these only in the sort of way in which any one of them differs from any other" (Collingwood, 5).

3. In his study of aesthetics in German philosophy, Jean-Marie Schaeffer summarizes the new aesthetic position in this way: "In the most fundamental manner it was thought that its (art's) essence had been found in a cognitive status which, not only would be specific to it, but would make of it at once the foundational knowledge and the knowledge of foundations" (Schaeffer, 15). The translation is my own.

4. One early twentieth-century reaction against "Art" developed in Japan. The Mingei Undo, a movement for the popular arts was championed vigorously by Yanagi Soetsu in writings and via the establish-

ment of a museum for the popular arts. Soetsu espoused a theory which articulated "new aesthetic criteria according to which objects are admirable to the degree in which they blend beauty and function, matter and spirit" (Frolet, 13). The translation is my own. For a dissenting view, one criticizing Malraux, see Gombrich.

5. For signalling the importance of Malraux, and for many other insights which have influenced this chapter, I owe a great debt to Thomas Alexander. See especially Alexander, 1987a.

6. Kant, the previous century's greatest thinker, had left open the possibility for a nonessentialist understanding of art by his refusal to subsume aesthetic judgments to cognitive ones. In his study of the aesthetics of the last three centuries, Jean-Marie Schaeffer explains this untapped possibility. The Kantian emphasis on the specific character of aesthetic judgment, when applied to the arts "renders cognitively null any philosophical doctrine based on a definition of the essence of art, and limits esthetic discourse to the evaluative critique of works, and (I would add) the the study of their phenomenal structures. Romanticism—and all of which followed it—short circuited the *Critique of Judgment* by a reduction of the Beautiful to the True and by its identification of esthetic experience with the presentation of an ontological content" (Schaeffer, 23, transation is my own).

7. For Hegel, Drama was the highest form of poetry, itself the highest of the arts. "Its words, which need not be sounded aloud or written, are signs addressed directly to our imaginative intelligence, where they are able, as Hegel expressed it, to produce the effects of all the other arts without the material means" (Paolucci, xii). On Schopenhauer, see *The World as Will and Representation*, vol. I, par. 52. Heidegger's views are succinctly expressed in "The Origin of the Work of Art": "The nature of art is poetry. The nature of poetry, in turn, is the founding of truth" (Heidegger, 1971, 75). For Kandinsky, the painter acts directly on the soul. "Generally speaking, color directly influences the soul. Color is the keyboard, the eyes are the hammers, the soul is the piano with many strings. The artist is the hand that plays, touching one key or another purposively, to cause vibrations in the soul" (Kandinsky, 44).

8. For example, the controversy between the sculptor Richard Serra and the office workers who resented the way his sculpture *Tilted Arc* interfered with their public space. See Tompkins, 181–87.

9. The most spirited, Deweyan-influenced, defense of popular art is to be found in Richard Shusterman's *Pragmatist Aesthetics*, especially in chapter 7.

7. Devotion

1. The last pages of both *Reconstruction in Philosophy* and *Human Nature and Conduct* offer meditations that are explicitly religious. The *Quest for Certainty* and *Art as Experience* are interspersed with suggestive comments on religion. *A Common Faith*, the Terry Lectures at Yale delivered in 1934, developed out of a review Dewey had written of *Is There a God? A Conversation* and the subsequent interchange between himself and the authors of this book. The review and some of the interchange are reprinted in LW 9.

2. I am grateful to Doug Anderson for unearthing this letter and for sharing it in a paper delivered to the Society for the Advancement of American Philosophy. Anderson's essay, "Theology as Healing: A Meditation on *A Common Faith*," is a sensitive reading of Dewey which will be published by SUNY Press in the collection *Democracy and the Aesthetics of Intelligence: New Essays in Deweyan Reconstruction*, edited by David I. Seiple.

3. Cf. "The religious experience is a reality in so far as in the midst of effort to foresee and regulate future objects we are sustained and expanded in feebleness and failure by the sense of an enveloping whole" (MW 14:181).

4. Cp. the comment of William James: "Luther, says Emerson, would have cut off his right hand rather than nail his theses to the door at Wittenberg, if he had supposed that they were destined to lead to the pale negations of Boston Unitarianism" (James, 1985, 265).

5. Cf. "If not, Mr. Wieman's argument would seem to me to amount simply to a plea that in a time of transition and disturbance many persons will find it helpful and consoling to continue to use the *word* 'God' to designate what actually are a collection of forces, unified only in their functional effect: the furtherance of goods in human life. This is an intelligible position; intelligent and honest persons will differ among themselves as to the desirability of carrying over the *term* God" (LW 9:220–21).

6. See quotation in note three above.

7. This comes out especially when Dewey gets effusive in his praise of Francis Bacon. See for example, MW 11:106–7, and MW 7:332.

8. See also Dykhuizen, 22.

8. Conclusion

1. Dewey admitted, that, in a loose sense at least, his philosophical positions held together in a systematic way (LW 14:141–42). This

dimension of Dewey's philosophy is rejected by Richard Rorty, representing the postmodern point of view. "I myself would join Reichenbach in dismissing classical Husserlian phenomenology, Bergson, Whitehead, the Dewey of *Experience and Nature*, the James of *Radical Empiricism*, neo-Thomist epistemological realism, and a variety of other late nineteenth- and early twentieth-century systems" (Rorty, 1982, 213–14).

2. Cp. "Poets who have sung of despair in the midst of prosperity, and of hope amid darkest gloom, have been the true metaphysicians of nature" (LW 1:96).

3. "But if modern tendencies are justified in putting art and creation first, then the implications of this position should be avowed and carried through. It would then be seen that science is an art, that art is practice, and that the only distinction worth drawing is not between practice and theory, but between those modes of practice that are not intelligent, not inherently and immediately enjoyable, and those which are full of enjoyed meanings. When this perception dawns, it will be a commonplace that art—the mode of activity that is charged with meanings capable of immediately enjoyed possession—is the complete culmination of nature, and that 'science' is properly a handmaiden that conducts natural events to this happy issue" (LW 1:268–69).

4. Cf. "Suppose we take seriously the contribution made to our idea of experience by biology,—not that recent biological science discovered the facts, but that it has so emphasized them that there is no longer an excuse for ignoring them or treating them as negligible. Any account of experience must now fit into the consideration that experiencing means living; and that living goes on in and because of an environing medium, not in a vacuum. Where there is experience, there is a living being" (MW 10:6–7). For an alternative reading of Dewey as best interpreted via technological metaphors, see Hickman.

5. On the importance of "root metaphors" for inspiring and distinguishing various philosophical positions, see Pepper.

Bibliography

Critical Edition of Works by Dewey:

EW *John Dewey: The Early Works: 1882–1898*, ed. Jo Ann Boydston, 5 vols. Carbondale and Edwardsville: Southern Illinois University Press, 1969–72.

MW *John Dewey: The Middle Works: 1899–1924*, ed. Jo Ann Boydston, 15 vols. Carbondale and Edwardsville: Southern Illinois University Press, 1976–83.

LW *John Dewey: The Later Works: 1925–1953*, ed. Jo Ann Boydston, 17 vols. Carbondale and Edwardsville: Southern Illinois University Press, 1981–90.

Major Dewey Books by Title

Art as Experience (1934) in LW 10.

A Common Faith (1934) in LW 9.

Democracy and Education (1916) in MW 9.

Experience and Education (1938) in LW 13.

Experience and Nature (1925, rev. ed. 1929) in LW 1.

How We Think (1910, rev. ed. 1933) in LW 8.

Human Nature and Conduct (1922) in MW 14.

Individualism Old and New (1930), in LW 5.

Logic: The Theory of Inquiry (1938) in LW 12.

Liberalism and Social Action (1935) in LW 11.

The Public and Its Problems (1927) in LW 2.

The Quest for Certainty (1929) in LW 4.

Reconstruction in Philosophy (1920, rev. ed. 1948) in MW 12.

Works by Others

Alexander, Thomas (1987a). *John Dewey's Theory of Art, Experience, and Nature.* Albany: SUNY Press.

—————. (1987b). "Art As Care." Paper presented at the Taos Aesthetics Institute, May 26.

Allen, Gay Wilson (1981). *Waldo Emerson: A Biography.* New York: Viking Press.

Anderson, Douglas (1996). "Theology as Healing: A Meditation on *A Common Faith.*" Paper presented at the annual meeting of the Society for the Advancement of American Philosophy, Toronto, March 8, 1996.

Aristotle (1984). *The Complete Works.* Ed. Jonathan Barnes. Princeton: Princeton University Press.

Ayer, Alfred J. (1952). *Language, Truth and Logic.* New York: Dover Publications.

Bacon, Francis ([1620] 1994). *Novum Organum.* Trans. and eds. Peter Urbach and John Gibson. Chicago: Open Court.

Barber, Elizabeth Wayland (1994). *Women's Work.* New York: W. W. Norton.

Baumgarten, Alexander Gottlieb ([1735] 1954). *Reflections on Poetry.* Trans. Karl Aschenbrenner and William Holther. Berkeley: University of California Press.

Bell, Clive (1949). *Art.* 2nd ed. London: Chatto & Windus.

Bellah, Robert, Richard Madsen, William Sullivan, Anne Swidler, Steven Tipton (1986). *Habits of the Heart.* New York: Perennial Library.

—————. (1991). *The Good Society.* New York: Alfred A. Knopf.

Belting, Hans (1994). *Likeness and Presence: A History of the Image before the Era of Art.* Trans. Edmund Jephcott. Chicago: University of Chicago Press.

Boisvert, Raymond (1988). *Dewey's Metaphysics.* New York: Fordham University Press.

—————. (1993). "Heteronomous Freedom." In *Philosophy and the Reconstruction of Culture: Pragmatic Essays after Dewey,* ed. John Stuhr. Albany: SUNY Press.

—————. (1997, forthcoming). "The Nemesis of Necessity: Tragedy's Challenge to Deweyan Pragmatism." In *Democracy and the*

Aesthetics of Intelligence: New Essays in Deweyan Reconstruction,
ed. David Seiple. Albany: SUNY Press.

Burke, Tom (1994). *Dewey's New Logic: A Reply to Russell.* Chicago:
University of Chicago Press.

Burnyeat, M. F. (1979). "Conflicting Appearances." *Proceedings of the
British Academy* 65: 69–111.

Burtt, Edwin A. (1960). "The Core of Dewey's Way of Thinking." *The
Journal of Philosophy* 57: 401–419.

Campbell, James (1995). *Understanding John Dewey.* LaSalle, Ill.: Open
Court.

Camus, Albert (1956). *The Rebel: An Essay on Man in Revolt.* Trans. A.
Brower. New York: Vintage Books.

Caputo, John (1987). *Radical Hermeneutics.* Bloomington: Indiana
University Press.

Clifford, W. K. ([1879] 1992). "The Ethics of Belief." In *Readings in the
Philosophy of Religion, An Analytic Approach,* ed. Baruch Brody.
2nd ed. Englewood Cliffs, N.J.: Prentice Hall.

Cohen, Carl, ed. (1962). *Communism, Fascism, and Democracy.* New
York: Random House.

Collingwood, R. G. ([1938] 1972). *The Principles of Art.* Oxford: Oxford
University Press.

Coughlan, Neil (1973). *Young John Dewey: An Essay in American
Intellectual History.* Chicago: University of Chicago Press.

Culp, Christopher (1992). *The End of Epistemology: Dewey and his
Current Allies on the Spectator Theory of Knowledge.* Westport,
Conn.: Greenwood Press.

Deleuze, Gilles and Felix Guattari (1991). *Qu'est-ce que la philosophie?*
Paris: Éditions de Minuit.

Descartes, René (1980). *Discourse on Method and Meditations on First
Philosophy.* Trans. Donald A. Cress. Indianapolis, Ind.: Hackett.

Descartes, Rene (1985). *The Philosophical Writings of Descartes, Vol. 1.*
Trans. J. Cottingham, R. Stoothoff, and Dugald Murdoch.
Cambridge: Cambridge University Press.

Diggins, John Patrick (1994). *The Promise of Pragmatism: Modernism
and the Crisis of Knowledge and Authority.* Chicago: University of
Chicago Press.

Dye, Thomas R., and L Harmon Zeigler (1975). *The Irony of Democracy: An Uncommon Introduction to American Politics.* 3d ed. No. Scituate, Mass.: Duxbury Press.

Dykhuizen, George (1973). *The Life and Mind of John Dewey.* Carbondale: Southern Illinois University Press.

Eco, Umberto (1983). *In The Name of the Rose.* Trans. William Weaver. New York: Warner Books.

————. (1984). *Postscript to the Name of the Rose.* Trans. William Weaver. New York: Harcourt Brace Jovanovich.

Eddington, Arthur S. (1929). *The Nature of the Physical World.* New York: Macmillan.

Edman, Irwin (1955). *The Uses of Philosophy: An Irwin Edman Reader,* ed. Charles Frankel. New York: Simon & Schuster.

Frolet, Élisabeth (1986). *Yanagi Soetsu ou les éléments d'une renaissance artistique japonaise.* Paris: Publications de la Sorbonne.

Geiger, George Raymond (1958). *John Dewey in Perspective.* New York: Oxford University Press.

Gellner, Ernest (1981). "Pragmatism and the Importance of Being Earnest." In *Pragmatism: its Sources and Prospects,* ed. Robert J. Mulvaney and Philip M. Zeltner. Columbia: University of South Carolina Press.

Glassie, Henry (1994). *Turkish Traditional Art Today.* Bloomington: Indiana University Press.

Gombrich, Ernst (1963). "André Malraux and the Crisis of Expressionism." In *Meditations on a Hobby Horse, and Other Esssays on the Theory of Art.* London: Phaidon Press.

Gouinlock, James (1986). *Excellence in Public Discourse: John Stuart Mill, John Dewey, and Social Intelligence.* New York: Teachers College Press.

Hartshorne, Charles and Paul Weiss, eds. (1934). *Collected Papers of Charles S. Peirce.* Cambridge, Mass.: Harvard University Press.

Hegel, Georg W. F. ([1807] 1979). *Phenomenology of Spirit.* Trans. A. V. Miller. Oxford: Oxford University Press.

Heidegger, Martin ([1950] 1971). "The Origin of the Work of Art." In *Poetry, Language, Thought.* Trans. Albert Hofstadter. New York: Perennial Library.

———. ([1938] 1977). "The Age of the World Picture." In *The Question Concerning Technology and Other Esssays*. Trans. William Lovitt. New York: Garland Publishing.

Hickman, Larry (1990). *John Dewey's Pragmatic Technology*. Bloomington: Indiana University Press.

———. (1991). "Review of *Dewey's Metaphysics* by Raymond D. Boisvert." *The Review of Metaphysics* 45: 112–14.

Holloway, Harry and John George (1979). *Public Opinion: Coalitions, Elites, and Masses*. 2nd ed. New York: St. Martin's Press.

James, William ([1890] 1950). *The Principles of Psychology, vol. 1*. New York: Dover Publications.

———. ([1902] 1985). *The Varieties of Religious Experience*. Cambridge, Mass.: Harvard University Press.

———. ([1907] 1981). *Pragmatism*. Indianapolis, Ind.: Hackett.

Jonas, Hans (1954). "The Nobility of Sight." *Philosophy and Phenomenological Research* 14: 507–19.

Kandinsky, Wassily ([1912] 1947). *Concerning the Spiritual in Art and Painting in Particular*. Trans. Michael Sadleir, rev. Francis Golffing, Michael Harrison, and Ferdinand Ostertag. New York: Wittenborn, Schultz.

Kaufman-Osborne, Timothy (1991). *Politics/Sense/Experience: A Pragmatic Inquiry into the Promise of Democracy*. Ithaca, N.Y.: Cornell University Press.

Kant, Immanuel ([1787] 1965). *Critique of Pure Reason*. Trans. Norman Kemp Smith. New York: St. Martin's Press.

Laertius, Diogenes (1950). *Lives of Eminent Philosophers*. Trans. R. D. Hicks. Cambridge, Mass.: Loeb Classical Library.

Latour, Bruno (1991). *Nous n'avons jamais été modernes: Essai d'anthropologie symétrique*. Paris: Éditions de la Découverte.

Lippmann, Walter (1925). *The Phantom Public*. New York: Harcourt, Brace and Co.

———. ([1922] 1965). *Public Opinion*. New York: The Free Press.

Locke, John ([1690] 1970). *Two Treatises of Government*. Ed. Peter Laslett. Cambridge: Cambridge University Press.

Macquarrie, John (1983). *In Search of Humanity: A Theological and Philosophical Approach*. New York: Crossroad.

Madison, James ([1787] 1983). "Federalist No. 10." In *Great American Political Thinkers*, vol. 1, ed. Bernard E. Brown. New York: Avon Books.

Malraux, André (1967). *Museum without Walls*. Trans. Stuart Gilbert and Francis Pride. Garden City, N.Y.: Doubleday.

Michels, Robert ([1911] 1966). *Political Parties: A Sociological Study of the Oligarchical Tendencies of Modern Democracy*. New York: The Free Press.

Mbiti, John (1970). *African Religions and Philosophy*. New York: Anchor Books.

Murray, Albert ([1976]1989). *Stomping the Blues*. New York: Da Capo Press.

————. (1996). *The Blue Devils of Nada*. New York: Pantheon Books.

Niebuhr, Reinhold (1932). *Moral Man and Immoral Society*. New York: Scribners.

Nussbaum, Martha C. (1986). *The Fragility of Goodness*. Cambridge: Cambridge University Press.

Ortega y Gasset, José (1971). *The Idea of Principle in Leibnitz and the Evolution of Deductive Theory*. Trans. Mildred Adams. New York: W. W. Norton.

————. (1932). *The Revolt of the Masses*. New York: W. W. Norton.

Paolucci, Henry (1979). *Hegel on the Arts*. New York: Frederick Ungar.

Padel, Ruth (1993). *In and Out of the Mind: Greek Images of the Tragic Self*. Princeton, N.J.: Princeton University Press.

Peirce, Charles Sanders (1955). *Philosophical Writings of Peirce*. Ed. Justus Buchler. New York: Dover Publications.

Pepper, Stephen (1942). *World Hypotheses: A Study in Evidence*. Berkeley: University of California Press.

Poe, Edgar Allan ([1845] 1976). *The Purloined Letter*. In *The Short Fiction of Edgar Allan Poe*, ed. Stuart and Susan Levine. Indianapolis, Ind.: Bobbs-Merrill.

Popper, Karl (1965). *Conjectures and Refutations*. New York: Basic Books.

Proust, Marcel (1934). *Swann's Way*. Trans. C. K. Scott Moncrieff. New York: Random House.

Randall, John Herman Jr. (1968). *The Meaning of Religion for Man*. New York: Harper Torchbooks.

Rescher, Nicholas (1985). "Philosophy in Academia." *American Philosophical Quarterly* 22: 155.

Rockefeller, Stephen (1991). *John Dewey: Religious Faith and Democratic Humanism*. New York: Columbia University Press.

Rorty, Richard (1979). *Philosophy and the Mirror of Nature*. Princeton, N.J.: Princeton University Press.

——— . (1980). "Pragmatism, Relativism, and Irrationalism." *Proceedings and Addresses of the American Philosophical Association* 53: 719–38.

——— . (1982). *Consequences of Pragmatism*. Minneapolis: University of Minnesota Press.

Ryan, Alan (1995). *John Dewey and the High Tide of American Liberalism*. New York: W. W. Norton.

Ruskin, John ([1871–72] 1904). *Modern Painters*, vols. 3–4. London: Everyman Library.

Russell, Bertrand ([1912] 1959). *The Problems of Philosophy*. Oxford: Oxford University Press.

Schaeffer, Jean-Marie (1992). *L'art de l'age moderne: L'esthétique et la philosophie de l'art du XVIIe siècle jusqu'à nos jours*. Paris: Gallimard.

Schopenhauer, Arthur ([1844] 1969). *The World as Will and Representation*, vol. 1. 2nd ed. Trans. E. F. J. Payne. New York: Dover Publications.

Serres, Michel (1992). *Éclaircissements*. Paris: Francois Bourin.

Shea, William M. (1984). *The Naturalists and the Supernatural*. Macon, Ga.: Mercer University Press.

Shusterman, Richard (1992). *Pragmatist Aesthetics: Living Beauty, Rethinking Art*. Oxford: Blackwell.

Sidorsky, David (1984). "Introduction" to LW 3.

Sleeper, Ralph (1986). *The Necessity of Pragmatism: John Dewey's Conception of Philosophy*. New Haven, Conn.: Yale University Press.

Smith, John. (1992). *America's Philosophical Vision*. Chicago: University of Chicago Press.

Tiles, J. E. (1988). *Dewey*. New York: Routledge.

De Tocqueville, Alexis ([1835, 1840] 1956). *Democracy in America*. Ed. Richard Heffner. New York: Mentor Books.

Tolstoy, Leo ([1898] 1975). "What is Art." In *What is Art and Essays on Art by Leo Tolstoy*. Trans. Aylmer Maude. London: Oxford University Press.

Tomkins, Calvin (1988). *Post- to Neo-: The Art World of the 1980's*. New York: Penguin Books.

Toulmin, Stephen (1984). "Introduction" to LW 4.

Tu, Wei-Ming (1983). "The Idea of the Human in Mencian Thought: An Approach to Chinese Aesthetics." In *Theories of the Arts in China*, ed. Susan Bush and Christian Murck. Princeton, N.J.: Princeton University Press.

Wallas, Graham (1914). *The Great Society: A Psychological Analysis*. New York: Macmillan.

West, Cornel (1989). *The American Evasion of Philosophy: A Genealogy of Pragmatism*. Madison: University of Wisconsin Press.

Westbrook, Robert (1991). *John Dewey and American Democracy*. Ithaca, N.Y.: Cornell University Press.

Wilde, Oscar ([1891] 1985). *The Picture of Dorian Gray*. London: Penguin Books.

Winthrop, John ([1630] 1987). "A Modell of Christian Charity." In *Individualism and Commitment in American Life*, ed. Robert Bellah et al. New York: Harper & Row.

Wittgenstein, Ludwig (1953). *Philosophical Investigations*. Trans. G. E. M. Anscombe. New York: Macmillan.

Index